General Counsel in the 21st Century: Challenges and Opportunities

Second Edition

EDITED BY E. LEIGH DANCE AND
CHRISTOPH H. VAAGT

Consulting editors
E. Leigh Dance and Christoph H. Vaagt

Managing director
Sian O'Neill

General Counsel in the 21st Century: Challenges and Opportunities, Second Edition
is published by

Globe Law and Business Ltd
3 Mylor Close
Horsell
Woking
Surrey GU21 4DD
United Kingdom
Tel: +44 20 3745 4770
www.globelawandbusiness.com

General Counsel in the 21st Century: Challenges and Opportunities, Second Edition

ISBN 9781787428638
EPUB ISBN 9781787428645
Adobe PDF ISBN 9781787428652

Contents

Part 3: Adding value and managing change

Executive summary

If a corporate legal leader back in 1995 heard today's general counsel describe his job role, she would shrug in disbelief. "How could you possibly handle all that?" she might ask. While many general counsel struggle with work–life balance in this highly demanding role, they also relish their increasingly strategic role in the business. General counsel today are often asked for input on decisions to drive company growth and avoid damaging wrong turns.

The 21st century legal leader must be alert to political socio-economic developments that might create reputational risks for the enterprise and change regulatory enforcement. They must often understand and advise on a vast range of new products and services. Many general counsel prioritize meeting key stakeholders' expectations above satisfying company shareholders.

Globe Law and Business published the first edition of the *General Counsel in the 21st Century* in 2015 in response to elevation of the position in companies and demands on in-house legal leaders to develop new competencies.

Seven years later, many of those demands remain and new ones are being continually added, ranging from digital transformation to the rigors of cybersecurity and from ESG and stakeholder governance to the GC's need to know how to keep a hybrid or remote legal team engaged.

For this second edition, we invited some of the best and the brightest in the legal sector to write chapters that will give you perspectives, particulars, and practical insights. We are enormously grateful to those contributors who took valuable time from their busy jobs to share some of their expertise and experience with their peers. Whilst not every single topic may be relevant to you, most will (and some may be arriving at your doorstep very soon!). We're confident that this book will give you valuable content along with lots of food for thought and application.

You will find both new developments and classic challenges that we think are relevant to corporate legal leaders today, grouped as follows:

- Part 1: Strategy and structure.
- Part 2: Leadership skills for the general counsel.
- Part 3: Adding value and managing change.

Without further ado, time to turn the page! There is no consecutive order. Browse and find what you need first. We welcome your comments.

Sincerely, your co-editors

E. Leigh Dance, consultant, founder and executive director, Global Counsel Leaders
Christoph H. Vaagt, managing partner, Law Firm Change Consultants

About the authors

Hans Albers is director, legal management consulting at Deloitte Legal where he is responsible for expanding Deloitte's legal management consulting practice by developing new capabilities and skills and building on Deloitte Legal's existing technology, change, and operations teams. Hans has extensive experience in legal process improvement, legal technology, legal operations, contract life cycle management, and outside counsel and spend management. Until October 2020, Hans was chief of staff and head of worldwide legal operations at US Technology company Juniper Networks Inc. Before that he was EMEA general counsel for Juniper as well as for Cisco EMEA and North America. He also served five years on the European Board of ACC (Association of Corporate Counsel), the last two years of which as president. Hans is also a non-executive director at Currencycloud, a fintech company that is part of the Visa group of companies.

Bruno Cova is a partner of Delfino Willkie Farr & Gallagher in Milan, Italy. His practice is a combination of transactional and litigation, focused on restructurings and corporate crises. He regularly acts for the boards of directors of international corporations and financial institutions in dealing with legal risks, devising internal controls or contractual mechanisms to minimize those risks, investigating legal and compliance problems, and defending clients before regulatory authorities or in the context of criminal investigations. Before returning to private practice, Bruno was general counsel of the exploration and production division of Eni, group general counsel at Fiat, chief compliance officer of the EBRD, and chief counsel to the extraordinary commissioner appointed by the Italian government to investigate Europe's largest financial fraud at Parmalat. He is member of the Advisory Board of the Anti-Corruption Committee of the International Bar Association and member of the troika of experts advising the Corporate Governance Committee of the Italian stock exchange.

Based in New York and Brussels, **E. Leigh Dance** is founder and executive director of Global Counsel Leaders, a forum of general counsel and compliance leaders. Members in greater Europe and North America include AB In-Bev, Accenture, AIG, Boston Consulting Group, Coca-Cola, DXC Technology, Jabil, Kingfisher, Koch Industries, KPMG UK, Smiths Group, Tenneco, Volvo Financial Services and others. Leigh also leads ELD International LLC, a consultancy she founded to support corporate legal teams to adapt best practices, manage change, improve team performance, service delivery, governance, crisis management, communications, professional development, and bespoke strategic projects. Recognized as a thought leader, Leigh's articles on issues facing general counsel and their teams have appeared in *The Wall Street Journal*, *Financial Times*, *American Lawyer*, and *Legal Week*. Leigh's book, *Bright Ideas: Insights from Legal Luminaries Worldwide*, includes 26 original essays by industry leaders. She writes regularly on international issues for *Corporate Counsel*.

William L. Deckelman, Jr is executive vice president and general counsel of DXC Technology Company. DXC was formed through the merger of CSC and the Enterprise Services business of HPE in 2017 and is headquartered in Ashburn, Virginia. William joined CSC as vice president and general counsel in 2008. Prior to joining CSC, he served as executive vice president and general counsel of Affiliated Computer Services, Inc. in Dallas, Texas, from 2000 through 2007. William began his legal career with Winstead, Sechrest & Minick in 1982 and subsequently was associated as in-house counsel with EDS and ACS. He opened the Austin, Texas office of Munsch Hardt in 1996 and was a partner with the firm until returning to ACS in 2000. William received his J.D., with Honors, in 1981 from the University of Arkansas School of Law where he was a member of the Arkansas Law Review. In 2014 he received an LLM, with Distinction, in International Business and Economic Law from Georgetown University Law Center, and an executive LLM in International Law from LSE Law, the London School of Economics, in 2021.

Maja Fabula is vice president and deputy general counsel for Tenneco Inc., a global manufacturing company headquartered in Skokie, Illinois. Prior to joining Tenneco, Maja was a partner with the law firm Kirkland & Ellis LLP, where her practice focused on antitrust defence, corporate internal investigations, and complex commercial litigation.

Kenneth J. Fredeen was general counsel and secretary to the board, Deloitte LLP (Canada), from 2000 to 2020. In his final year in the partnership, he was appointed general counsel emeritus and senior partner, indigenous and accessibility, leading Deloitte's reconciliation and disability initiatives. In June 2021, he retired from the partnership. A recognized leader in the legal profession, Ken was named Canada's Outstanding General Counsel in 2018 and in 2021 he received the Canadian Corporate Counsel Association R.V.A. Jones Award and the Lifetime Achievement Award by the Canadian General Counsel Awards. Ken has spent over two decades supporting a more diverse and inclusive legal profession in Canada and has received numerous awards for his DEI efforts, including the SABA Diversity Award, the David C. Onley Award for his work related to creating a more inclusive Canada for people with disabilities, Catalyst Canada Business Leader Award, and the Leading Executive Ally Award by Leaders to be Proud Of.

Leanne Geale was appointed executive vice president, general counsel, corporate governance and compliance, and a member of the Executive Board of Nestlé S.A. on 1 August 2019. Prior to that Leanne had been the chief ethics and compliance officer of Royal Dutch Shell plc from 2014 to 2019, having joined Shell Canada in 2003. At Shell, she held the positions of associate general counsel, oil products, group legal services coordinator, and associate general counsel, heavy oil and head of legal – Canada. Prior to joining Shell, Leanne had been in-house counsel for international, publicly listed companies in the banking (Royal Bank of Canada), mining (Rio Algom Limited), and manufacturing (Alcan Aluminium Limited) sectors. Leanne is a member of the board of directors of Holcim Ltd and the CEELI Institute o.p.s. based in Prague whose mission is advancing the rule of law. Leanne has been an active volunteer in the areas of mental illness and diversity and inclusion. Born and raised in Canada, Leanne holds a B.A. from the University of Alberta and a LL.B. from the Université de Montréal.

Dr Wolf-Peter Gross is management consultant at Law Firm Change Consultants, the leading consulting firm for law firms and legal departments in Europe. He is a lawyer, systemic organizational consultant, leadership coach, and business mediator. He was chief legal officer in the telecommunication and system integration industry and has many years of experience as managing director in international businesses. Since 2005, Wolf-Peter has been a consultant with a focus on strategy, organisation, operations, and change in professional service firms and law departments. Wolf-Peter is the author of several books and articles.

Susan Hackett, CEO of Legal Executive Leadership, LLC, (LEL) is a recognized leader in building smarter legal practices, with over three decades of experience helping law departments (and those who serve them) deliver distinguishing value and improve the way they work. She formed Legal Executive Leadership after serving for 22 years as the SVP and GC of the Association of Corporate Counsel (ACC). Using her platform, Susan helps clients develop and implement change strategies for the future, improve operational processes, drive demonstrable client results, and move confidently from traditional practice toward legal executive leadership.

Christian Lawrence is a partner at Brunswick Group's Munich office. Before joining Brunswick, he was head of group communications for Munich Re. Prior to working for Munich Re he has served in leading communications positions in Germany, the US, and the UK. At Munich Re, Christian helped steer the company's reputation through the financial crisis and supported its transformation from a pure supplier of reinsurance capacity to a vendor of digital insurance solutions for primary insurers. One of his core competencies is to help traditional communication departments to identify and engage with influencers on digital platforms. Prior to his work at Munich Re, Christian was responsible for internal and external communications at Allianz Global Investors, was head of global communications at General Reinsurance, a subsidiary of Berkshire Hathaway based in Stamford, Connecticut, and he spent eight years with the German automotive supplier Bosch, where he held various positions. Among them he was the head of communications of its UK subsidiary, Robert Bosch Ltd, in London. Christian holds a doctorate in law.

Dr Robert Loef is a seasoned and versatile corporate M&A lawyer with high business acumen, expansive leadership experience, and a focus on capital markets. He currently serves as group general counsel of Best Secret Group AG, a private equity owned leading European members-only online destination for premium and luxury off-price fashion. Prior to this, he led the corporate law, M&A, and commercial legal department of ProSiebenSat.1 Media SE, Germany's leading TV broadcasting group listed in the M-Dax. Before going in-house, Robert practiced as an external corporate and M&A lawyer in an international law firm in New York and Munich. Robert was nominated a Young Leader by the American Counsel on Germany, ACG (2011), and held various positions in US-European legal associations, e.g., vice president of the American Foreign Law Association.

Áine Lyons is the SVP and deputy general counsel leading global legal operations, privacy, and international and commercial legal at VMware. She also serves as the chief of staff to VMware's general counsel. Working with the legal team and the business, she drives legal operational excellence through scalable innovation. Áine has over 20 years of experience managing legal and cross-functional teams in fast-moving technology companies. A founding member of the Women@VMware POD and a VMinclusion Strategy Council member for five years, Áine helped shape VMware's DEI strategy. She is an executive sponsor and member of the ESG Council and is passionate about operationalizing ESG to drive greater purpose and impact. She is on the board of the Corporate Legal Operations Consortium (CLOC), where she is a founding member, and is the CLOC Europe Lead, driving industry change and legal eco-system connection. *The Financial Times* named Áine the 2019 "Legal Intrapreneur of the Year" for her transformation efforts, and in 2022 named her in its list of "Champions of Legal Transformation". Her team has won multiple awards for operational excellence and driving industry change in how legal services are delivered.

Dr Anne Meckbach is an experienced in-house lawyer and compliance officer. She is currently chief compliance officer of ProSiebenSat.1 Group, Germany's leading TV broadcasting group listed in the M-Dax. Before turning to compliance, she gained vast experience in M&A and corporate law, working for the legal department of ProSiebenSat.1 and earlier in the M&A department of a large international law firm for more than a decade. Besides her in-house experience in the media industry, Anne also worked in-house for one of the world's largest quick service restaurant companies in the USA. She frequently gives presentations and publishes in various legal journals.

Isabel Parker has spent her career pushing boundaries and driving change in the legal profession. She has a particular interest in legal digital transformation and is currently the executive director of The Digital Legal Exchange, a global not-for-profit supporting leading corporations to accelerate the digital transformation of the corporate legal function. Before this, Isabel spent 24 years at leading law firm Freshfields Bruckhaus Deringer, as a finance lawyer and as chief legal innovation officer and head of knowledge, shaping the firm's digital transformation strategy. During her tenure, Freshfields was named the Most Innovative Law Firm in Europe in 2019. Isabel was herself listed as one of the top ten innovative lawyers in the FT

Innovative Lawyers Report for 2018 and as a winner in the professional services category in the European Women of Legal Tech Awards 2020. Isabel's first book, *Successful Digital Transformation in Law Firms: A Question of Culture*, was published by Globe Law and Business in November 2021.

As CEO of UnitedLex, **Daniel Reed** has a singular focus on empowering customers to achieve their own unique "art of the possible" in the field of law. As a former general counsel and CFO of public and private equity-backed companies, Dan identified the unexplored opportunity to transform legal and business data to yield business advantage. He saw the power of delivering holistic legal services through a revolutionary platform of technology and data science. Central to Dan's vision is UnitedLex's extreme customer centricity and commitment to outcomes with UnitedLex leaning in with significant "skin in the game". This vision has fueled UnitedLex's growth from a handful of employees in 2007 to a highly-skilled international workforce of over 3,000 lawyers, engineers, consultants, and technologists today. Dan earned his accounting degree from the University of Florida and his JD from Vanderbilt University. Ernst & Young named Dan its "Entrepreneur of the Year" in the Technology and Business Services category for the US Midwest Region.

Christoph H. Vaagt is the founder and managing partner of the consulting firm for law firms and legal departments, Law Firm Change Consultants, based in Munich, Germany. He holds a degree in law and has worked as a consultant for various industries and as a lawyer in Munich, before turning to the consulting of law firms and legal departments. Prior to the foundation of his own firm in 2005, he has been a consultant with Hildebrandt International, the major US law firm consultancy. Having worked with leading consultants such as Brad Hildebrandt and Alan Hodgart for leading US and UK law firms on projects ranging from devising international strategies to arranging mergers, he has acted with his consultants for major German, Austrian, Swiss, and continental Top 100 European firms. He has specialised in change management techniques, focusing on strategy and culture of law firms. Christoph is author of the first benchmark study of the German law firm market and has edited on behalf of the IBA the book *Law Firm Strategies for the 21st Century*, as well as contributed to German speaking publications on law firm management and legal department management.

Chapter 1: A slow motion riot – the evolving role of the general counsel and the legal department

By Susan Hackett, CEO, Legal Executive Leadership, LLC

Introduction

When Leigh Dance and Chris Vaagt asked me to contribute my thoughts on this topic to their updated edition of *General Counsel in the 21st Century,* I started rummaging through my mind and experiences for what I might offer. Working through all the bits and pieces made me realize that, somehow, I've spent over 30 years fully marinating in all things relevant to the in-house community. I am fortunate to have been a part of the extensive evolution of the role of the in-house legal team and general counsel – first through my work at ACC (the Association of Corporate Counsel), and more recently as a consultant. These last 30-some years have played host to the most significant and transformative changes ever for lawyering in general, and for practice by in-house leaders, in specific.

Most of these changes are very visible to those who watch in-house teams and those who work with them, but it's not as if there's a lot of statistically significant or academic documentation of the evolution of in-house practice – it's not easy to capture or measure. What exists is a variety of legal press covering people and events, some management studies, transcripts from programs purporting to explore the topic, and periodic surveying. And folks like me, whose profession is to watch and record. I'm fully aware that the very nature of evolution is that it is ongoing. Since the in-house community works in such a wide variety of organizations and includes hundreds of thousands of differently skilled practitioners, it's hard for anyone who's not studying it full-time to see the changing attributes of the forest when they're focused on the maturation of just a few of the trees at a time.

The progress of in-house teams has sometimes been driven and other times has been led by the wider changes in legal practice that started simmering and shaping in-house legal roles in the late 20th century and for these first two decades of the 21st. But the foundation for this in-house evolution – namely, the distinguishing features of in-house practice – made the evolution inevitable. I used to call the progress of the in-house bar a "slow motion riot". This chapter is about the riot that general counsel and legal teams seem to be promoting; but what will shine through is the importance of the pace of change and the difficulty of progress.

What makes in-house practice special?

It makes sense to begin with a reminder of what it is that distinguishes in-house practice and the role of the general counsel from all other types of legal practices. From their position as employed counsel, the first characteristic that stands out is that the in-house lawyer has one client – so the in-house leader can hone their focus and services to find a well-defined target. We all know that's a bit of an overstatement, since most businesses large enough to employ their own legal team have multiple operations and business lines, far-flung facilities and employees, and an array of corporate leaders and constituencies with whom to interact. But in representing a singular entity, the in-house counsel's "client" is actually the board of directors of the enterprise and the best interests of the company – not any of those individuals or issues that make up the company.

In representing the enterprise, the in-house lawyer who leverages their role can deliver unique value for their client by doing what others cannot (rather than by replicating what others can). These values include:

- A baseline of services that are delivered without waiting for someone to request them (or understand what is needed);
- Real-time engagement with business leaders as work is done and decisions are made;
- An ability to partner with the business to help advance its goals and successes;
- An array of risk and compliance services that help prevent problems from arising;
- A focus on delivering services in a manner that is consistent with the business' operational model and practices;
- A strong set of ongoing, institutional relationships that allow the counsellor to engage in matters immediately from a position of trust and alignment; and
- The management of retained providers, such as law firms, who provide services that the in-house team is not scaled to provide (such as litigation or M&A), or specialized expertise for non-repeating matters.

It is because of their unique position in leading in-house teams that general counsel are perfectly positioned (destined?) to leverage these values to create the kinds of charges we've seen in the last 30 to 40 years. Once seen as the lesser cousin to their brethren in leading law firms, GCs are now recognized as professional superpowers who influence and direct the provision of legal services in the marketplace. Indeed, it is clear that many are among the most highly visible, influential, digitally empowered, global executives in their companies, as well.

In the beginning...

Legal departments have been around for a long time – longer than most people realize. The first large corporate in-house teams were fully operational and visible in the mid-1800s in the US. They were slower to develop in other countries and companies around the world, but were soon present, even if not commonplace, in most developed corporate markets by the early 1900s.

Since there were few large law firms at that time in any part of the world, it could be presumed that many companies built the first in-house teams to create their own version of a full-service, captive law firm that couldn't yet be found in the market. In companies with only a few in-house lawyers, the GC nonetheless provided terrific value by not only providing some baseline services in-house, but also by relieving other businesspeople, who didn't understand the legal issues at play, of the need to retain and manage a passing parade of many small firms or individual specialists.

But while some of these reasons for building an in-house team are still valid, there are other reasons why companies then – and now – draw particular benefit from housing an in-house department. Foremost amongst them are:

- Institutional knowledge of the company's business, the clients they serve, and the industry marketplace, creating not only a trusted relationship, but the ability to avoid climbing a learning curve with each new matter;
- Cost savings, but even more importantly, cost control and predictability – instead of "spend until the matter is resolved" (or the company runs out of money);
- The need for transactional and recurring "business as usual" services (governance, employment issues, contracts, etc.). In the early days, not many law firms offered general services; they were specialists

or litigators. In more recent years, not many law firms of size could perform this work efficiently, or at a comparable price point to or with the results delivered by the in-house team;

- A focus on risk management and compliance counseling, especially as regulations on companies became more complex and numerous; and
- Trusted and candid counsel for top leaders in the company to advise on business issues from a perspective beyond what other leaders in the C-suite offer.

How the demographics of corporate legal practice shape this conversation

The most common misperception regarding in-house counsel is that there are a lot of them. In-house counsel constitute only about ten percent of the total number of lawyers – while there are a lot of lawyers out there (and many more than there used to be), the number of in-house lawyers in the lawyer population remains steady at a small minority, even as their visibility and influence grows. Why?

I'd suggest the following:

- Many companies with in-house lawyers have relatively small teams – solos or a few – even when the company is pretty sophisticated and of good size. For instance, more than half of the Fortune 500 and FTSE have an in-house legal team with fewer than 75 lawyers (working as lawyers). Only a fraction of those topping the Fortune and FTSE lists have more than 250 lawyers. So when we think about large legal teams that dominate the profession and its practices, let's remember that there are many more "super large" law firms than large legal departments.
- A lot of companies opt for a management model for their expense centers that outsources service provision. In other words, they choose not to hire a full service team of employees to provide internal services – they instead staff a group of experts who lead the service function and supervise the outsourcing of the majority of the work to "just-in-time/just-what's-needed" firms, consultants, or providers.
- The single largest "type" of law department is a solo GC. This isn't a surprise when you think of the number of companies that are start-ups or smaller businesses that only afford a single leader to

> staff the function as they get rolling. First hires in most companies don't include in-house lawyers – outside firms are retained initially and remain in that role until the company is well-established and staffing out the "cost" centers that will serve up insourced services. Of course, the presumption is that, over time, the department may grow as the company expands. But it will likely grow slowly – few companies triple the size of their in-house teams every few years as that's not generally how corporate staffing budgets work, regardless of the increased efficiency that a five- or 15- or 35-person department might offer over the solo lawyer the company currently employs.

So much attention is focused on what large law departments in very high-profile companies (and the large firms that serve them) are doing. We come to think of their practices and profiles as the "norm" for the market, business model, and value proposition. But while the "bigs" are terrific, I'm sure, they are not the norm, nor should they drive our perception of what is good and bad practice, since they are most likely to perform work "the way it's always been done", and least likely to change the way they think or deliver service. There's an old saying in the business world: "It's hard to convince a bunch of millionaires they're doing something wrong."

And we all know that clients pay handsomely for their large department and large law firm legal service providers to continue to do exactly what they've always done.

So I often find the most interesting and valuable practice changes happening in the smaller and mid-size law departments and the firms that serve them. Smaller teams are more flexible, more transparent, less able to bury waste or fails – and they have no time or staff to spare on less than the most efficient path. Even if the smaller in-house team can't do the bulk of the legal work for their company in-house, they still provide those strengths afforded by their distinguishing value; the company still enjoys counsel informed by their institutional knowledge of the needs and practices of the company, and they are far more likely to closely supervise and seek alignment or partnership in their retention and supervision of the outside counsel who do the rest. Many small department GCs aren't yet armed with a toolkit that allows them to focus on discounts on firms' rates, but an increasing number are exploring the much wider range of more effective partnering techniques that drive efficient and controlled-cost service provision. These small- and medium-sized departments are probably more likely to drive needed changes across the legal market than the bigs will be – the smalls can't afford the inefficiencies and waste that the bigs can pad into the fat of their business model's scale.

Striking the right balance between "make" versus "buy"

Whatever the "percentage" of work done in-house versus outside, outside counsel have always played a role as a necessary complement to in-house teams. I don't know of any company with an in-house legal team that doesn't also retain law firms to handle litigation, matters that require a lawyer in another jurisdiction, or issues that require specialized expertise that the company doesn't wish to add to its permanent roster. The average mid-size to larger legal department (depending on whether you're measuring spend or number and type of matters) usually sends a bit more than half of the company's legal work to outside firms. In smaller companies or departments, the percentages often demonstrate a much larger spread.

There's never really been a good measure or benchmark for how much work should stay inside with an in-house legal team, and how much should be outsourced. Many in-house counsel hire outside counsel because of capacity issues – they may not need particularly specialized expertise from them, but they just don't have the capacity to get any more work done internally, so everything beyond their tipping point is simply thrown over the wall to a law firm. Others send out everything that is included in a certain kind of work because of a lack of specialty in-house or insufficient scale to staff the work, and keep other things they feel they are best suited and sized to perform. There isn't a formula, nor do I think there ever will be, that suggests that in every company and department, this is what's right to keep in-house and that is what's right to send outside. That's as it should be.

But as each department tries to find its own best balance, they often are making decisions without any data or objective standards to guide them on how to make the split – they lack data or experience to assess comparative costs, efficiencies, or practice specialties. As I hope is becoming clearer, I don't believe the only reason to choose to keep versus outsource work should be driven solely or primarily by cost (as opposed to distinguishing value and results delivered). But most lawyers in general are blunt instruments in understanding the differences between the cost of service and the price of service, or the value of an outcome within a range of timeframes, or the savings and increased quality of output that could be accomplished through automation or better work process and staffing decisions. Most lawyers only have the prices charged by outside firms to define the "worth" of legal work in the marketplace (which is their price, not their worth or cost), and little to help us define the value of legal work to clients. We tend to define the value of legal services based on how lawyers perceive it, not based on how it is perceived and valued by the companies we serve.

Further, while the in-house counsel's distinguishing attributes drive great value of all kinds for clients, their value is often harder to define, nonetheless quantify, than that of those who are outside the company and submitting a bid and invoice for services. How do you book the value of the expense that the company avoided because the in-house legal team prevented a problem from occurring? How do you quantify the worth of advice that helps the company navigate its daily course?

Of greatest concern to me is the fact that it's easy to diminish the value of in-house work, especially since it isn't expensed (and therefore connected to a higher market value rate) the same way that outside firms' services are. Indeed, many companies don't even expense the cost of the internal legal team's work to the business units that benefit from it, or the projects they are supporting. The legal department budget offers services to every function and project in the company that needs their help, under the umbrella of a general service budget – even if allocated to different functions, it's rare for costs to be charged back.

So the highly valuable services provided by an in-house team don't come with a noticeable or even quantifiable price tag to their customers/consumers in the company. But legal services do come with a very significant price tag when billed by outside counsel when they lead the closure of a giant merger or conduct the internal investigation into a corporate fail. Further, in-house legal teams rarely get credit for their role in bringing home a windfall like the successful establishment of the business in a new market or a major award when there's a verdict in a case involving a bet-the-company matter won by an outside firm that was selected, supported, managed, and directed by the in-house team. While business-people and other lawyers should know better, many conflate law firms' higher costs with higher quality or greater value; that which you "don't pay for" is often presumed to be of lower value. Neither premise is true.

Why aren't GCs driving changes faster and farther than they are?

We all know that most general counsel and leading lawyers in law departments come from law firms. They and most everyone else believes that large and prestige law firm services are the gold standard – because they are large, they have lots of highly pedigreed and experienced lawyers, and they charge gold standard prices. But the upshot is that law firm lawyers who move in-house at all levels of seniority start their time in-house behaving like outside counsel and emulating their "gold standard" practices. Some never grow beyond that; others see a different path over time if they are lucky enough to work directly with businesspeople who teach them different ways to think and work. But the upshot is that departments are often led and populated by people who know they want to offer more business-savvy and efficient services, but are so embedded in lawyer-centric/law-firm-centric practices that they can't get out of their own way.

In fairness, most lawyers don't know how and often aren't being pressured to deliver their services any other way than the way they are trained in law firms. Law school or legal coursework in universities don't do much if anything to help – we are a profession that looks to the past to figure out where we should be going forward. Precedent rules!

The GC/in-house revolution is based on that slow-motion realization that how law firms practice law is probably driven by what is of greatest interest and value to lawyers who make their money working in law firms. As that realization sinks in, it's complemented by an increasing understanding that what clients think is important is not always the same thing as what lawyers think is important. When you work in an in-house legal team of two, 20, 200 or 2,000 in a company with tens, if not hundreds of thousands of businesspeople who define value differently, at some point you begin to examine why you think your minority view and business practices should prevail over the businesses'. And then your head truly explodes when you realize that how businesspeople from different disciplines solve problems or leverage their value can actually provide ideas and models for how to improve how lawyers solve problems or leverage their value. Ka-pow!

Whatever the reason, since law firms don't preach or practice efficiency and consistent work processes, or seek to implement performance standards that target results (instead of piling up hours and billings), the resulting spill-over impacts departments that rely on firms to perform the majority of their legal workload and also fill their ranks. It's only over time and with great attention to change practices that law departments learn that they have every financial, relationship, and functional incentive to drive this change in spite of how hard it will be to turn this particular battleship in this particular bathtub.

So how does the distinguishing value in-house team lead toward a better future in law?

It's my premise (and I'm joined by many others, I'm sure) that the greater value of the evolved legal department is its ability to harness outside firms for what outside firms do best, and to focus their own work on what only in-house teams can do best. The choice of work and the proportion of work done in-house versus outside should never be based on a law department replicating law firm services in-house, even if it's "cheaper" that way. In today's market of "cheaper" services, the in-house legal department is rarely the best cheaper option, even if it is cheaper and better than a more expensive outside law firm. Indeed, part of what is speeding that slow motion riot up is the entry of a variety of companies, service providers, and evolving technologies and process improvements that make every kind of lawyer more expensive, less efficient, and demonstrably less effective than these alternative providers. There is much that these providers and technologies don't do and maybe never will do that will remain the province of lawyers. But why would lawyers want to try to hold onto work others do better, rather than releasing the work to them, supervising and customizing it, and spending their time on what is their higher value to the client?

Law departments should set their agenda and strategy based on what it is that allows them to best leverage their distinguishing value. While there are hundreds or thousands of resources and service providers that can be deployed to offer good to great legal services of certain kinds to a corporate client, *a great law department is the opposite of fungible*. A great law department provides irreplaceable value to its client and is highly differentiated from other solution providers in the market; it's tightly focused on understanding and addressing the client's highest priority work and how to best deliver services that don't just protect their businesses, but partner with them to excel in the marketplace.

The lack of interest the legal profession has demonstrated throughout its history in offering services that are aligned with and valuable to their "customers" is the subject of another chapter. But it's an important conversation to reference here since our fundamental value and premise as a profession is to serve. If we don't serve what clients want, how they want it, and with a value that they recognize, eventually clients will find others who will. There were few alternatives ten years ago; there are thousands now, and they have established track records.

Regardless of lawyer regulation that seeks to prevent others from competing to provide legal services, corporate clients will find and hire or retain many varied and highly competent experts or providers who provide needed services or solve complex problems for them. (And so will individual clients looking for basic legal services that they can't afford to buy from lawyers in traditional practices, as well.)

None of this means that lawyers will have no value in the future. It just means that they will be strongly challenged by new market competition.

And this competition will challenge both in-house counsel and outside firms equally, because they currently perform the same kinds of services at a premium cost, in a marketplace that has created providers and technologies to perform the same work for far less money, in less time, and often with quantifiably better results from the perspective of the clients served.

The changing marketplace of legal service providers

Real change has come to the marketplace of choices for clients via an army of new service providers, technological solutions, and specialized offerings that take advantage of:

- Smart, highly trained workers (some of whom are lawyers and others who bring a variety of sophisticated skills and disciplines beyond the law);
- Lean and efficient processes and project management;
- Data, predictive analytics, and technology;
- Highly transparent operational and business models that mirror the models used by the businesses they serve; and
- Knowledge-based solutions (that avoid "re-inventing the wheel" with each iteration of the work).

What may be most challenging to traditional legal service providers like law firms and in-house counsel is that many corporate clients already know, use, and enjoy productive relationships with companies and technologies that provide this competition. Clients and consumers are already "sold" on the value proposition of some of these service providers (such as the Big Four, large consulting practices, or staffing firms such as Axiom). And many clients are very comfortable (even if their lawyers aren't) with automated solutions that replace the need for a traditional legal team, such as Legal Zoom or Rocket Lawyer, and a growing number of no-code process solutions for handling repetitive and relatively routine business needs or problems.

It will be interesting to see if change is shaped or accelerated by a new generation of evolved in-house leaders – general counsel or CLOs, as well as senior lieutenants on their leadership teams. I see a growing number of GCs and in-house team leaders who are focused on moving beyond the law firm model of service that values "the way we've always done it" over results delivered – for both their own work and the services they purchase from firms. Law departments and law firms are making some limited use of other service provider options that can support their businesses and practices, but many more aren't, or still view such services and technologies as a greater threat than a help-mate. That's a losing strategy – one that prevents most or all corporate lawyers from spending their time and talents on that which is of higher value, by freeing them from over-occupation with lower value or repeating work that could be done by others.

The challenges posed by old systems colliding with new markets, processes, and practices, and GCs who want to promote change

GCs who want to drive better practices and change the way their teams work often feel like salmon swimming upstream, struggling against the current, only to lay their eggs and die. Not only do they face an overwhelming preference and practice that values the traditional way of doing things (from both their in-house and outside counsel), they also face push-back and barriers erected by those who regulate the legal profession. Many already believe that all they can do is lay those eggs; true change will belong to the generations that follow, and follow through.

The profession and its regulators (the bars, the judiciary, the government) have a longstanding history of working hard to preserve the "way lawyers have always done it". The published rules of professional regulation and the decisions that flow from them are written to resist and diminish the value of lawyers embracing improved business processes and technology. They argue that it isn't professional to adopt practices that promote business efficiencies, and that lawyers who engage in collaborative and multi-disciplinary teams lack the independent judgment that professionalism requires. The rules ignore that probably 90 percent of what lawyers do is not about judgment or independent legal analysis, but simple process. And process is replicable by anyone or any system with the smarts, resources, and training to the task.

Current bar rules, professional regulation, and disciplinary opinions reflect a fundamental belief that good legal advice and analysis are inherently subjective and bespoke, and cannot be "knowledge-" or "process-managed". To argue otherwise, they say, opens the door to the idea that much of what lawyers do can be done by others with targeted training or a system to produce a consistent and desired result. This goes directly to my point; the challenge for lawyers is not to ignore or try to outlaw the reality that some of their services can be provided well by others, but to constantly move toward what it is that cannot be provided well by others or replicated by systems. Trust me, there's plenty of that better work that lawyers never got to because they're so busy trying to hold on to the sole authority to perform work that isn't our highest or best calling anymore.

In the US, there are a few state bars that have established commissions or working groups to explore changes to the rules to embrace and leverage change in the legal marketplace, but they are not going far or fast enough to outpace the change that's taking place in spite of what the profession decides to authorize or continues to outlaw.

The rising opportunity of the in-house team and general counsel to drive change in the marketplace

I remember a specific conversation with a GC whom I loved to work with from my days at ACC. He was a mentor and is what you might call a "serial GC"; he has worked in many different companies including a drug company and an airline. I jokingly asked him how he'd moved from pharma to airlines as a top lawyer since he knew nothing about airlines except how to find his seat when he boarded one. We laughed, but in the ensuing conversation, he explained that in his experience, savvy companies are no longer interested in hiring a top lawyer for their legal expertise, but for their ability to lead a team of legal experts who have to solve business problems. He said that when it comes to understanding airline legal needs, he – like his client – "has all kinds of people who can do that" for him. He relayed that the person the company wanted in the GC seat was someone who could deliver performance, predictability, integrity, and results in a highly regulated industry. That conversation changed how I thought about the best value of a general counsel; I still don't think you can define the evolving role of the leading GC any better.

While we don't have overwhelming change across the entire profession that we can measure yet, we do have overwhelming recognition of what is necessary to be relevant and valued in the future. Our future value as lawyers and trusted counselors is exactly what this mentor described as his role and value. To remain relevant, lawyers need to understand that practicing law is table stakes. Our higher role is as leaders, as aligned business executives, as multi-disciplinary problem solvers, as critical partners with clients, as engaged collaborators with highly expert specialists and teams.

Here we are, as of this writing, emerging from two-plus years of disruption and unprecedented challenges presented by a global pandemic. In-house teams emerging from the chaos are ironically more empowered to lead change than they may have been pre-pandemic. The need to shift immediately to remote practice required them to leave the traditional culture and traditional thinking that brought them to the party in favor of a culture and thinking that would lead them and their clients safely through a massive disruption and entity-threatening events.

It forced them to rely on technology and communications in a manner they'd never chosen. A lot of folks discovered, when the tide went out, just who was and wasn't wearing a swimsuit. The lasting impact has been to leave law departments and their leaders better prepared, more capable, confident, and effective than before – if they didn't have a swimsuit, they got one pretty quick. People who never paid attention to the conversation before were suddenly riveted. Was everyone completely and perfectly changed and reformed? No. But departments (and law firms, as well) that couldn't fathom the implementation of systems and platforms to improve process and collaboration found themselves knee-deep in implementing aggressive value practices.

So woe to the firms or departments who think that the better course now is to pretend that everything can revert to pre-2020 standards and practices. That ship has sailed.

Remote work and pandemic problems taught legal teams some very specific lessons – like the need to define and communicate legal team members' performance expectations and measure their contributions to articulated priorities. So many lawyers were accustomed to measuring performance by hours worked and piles of activities, rather than the outcomes they're asked to deliver. But once leaders lost sight of what and when people were doing the work as they logged in from their homes at all hours and working as they wished, the only thing that was important was the ability to ascertain that the tasks they were assigned were being accomplished, done right, and generated the intended result.

The pandemic also fast-tracked the process of moving lawyers and teams en masse and without exceptions onto platforms and into process flows that forced them to use communication and technology systems that connected them to others they previously saw in the hallway or emailed in more of an inconsistent or "drive-by" fashion. Perhaps most importantly, it built confidence that legal teams can work on systems virtually and succeed.

What I found most interesting was that a lot of the artificial and physical walls between outside providers, firms, and departments disappeared, making workflows far less dysfunctional. Online, issues of hierarchy that often slowed or made work less efficient fell by the wayside, as everyone joining the Zoom call had the same sized box and coordinated or reported in real time, together. Those usually revered as all-knowledgeable were asking juniors for help sharing their screens or understanding how a project might continue forward. Contributions to the work were judged by timely and successful completion, without regard for where workers sat, who employed or retained them, how they were paid for their contributions, and other distinctions that suddenly were without a difference. These successes also opened many teams to the idea that they might re-think their workflow processes and prioritize their service model based on better alignment with the client's needs, not on how lawyers have always organized themselves or how they prefer to perform tasks.

Is everyone onboard and loving it? Does everyone enjoy immediate and easy success? Of course not. While I know folks would like to flip a switch and have change be done, that's not how it works. The need to change and improve the department and the roles of its team members – inside the department, in outside law firms, and with legal service providers – is a never-ending journey. It's just a matter of whether the riot remains a riot, and whether it's in slow motion, or taking place in real-time, in order to be of value and relevance to our clients.

Going forward – how will GCs and in-house teams lead?

General counsel are discovering that it is their highest role and priority to lead the charge for change; their future role encompasses much more than just the performance of the legal and counseling services they've always delivered. For those in departments with more than a few lawyers, the role of the GC isn't to try to do it all herself, but to assure that the mission is articulated, a strategy developed, and individuals or teams are assigned and accountable for delivering results. The GC needs to assure those who take on change leadership roles that they will be rewarded for taking risks, demonstrating leadership, and owning their decisions. They need to publicly forgive failures that will occur since change is a process that requires creative experimentation and failure is a natural part of the process. But they also need to demonstrate commitment and resilience in the face of slow progress or fails because change requires teams that don't get it right the first time to learn from the fail and try again, and do better.

Law departments (and law firms) are "people" businesses. Their leaders who are in charge of driving change face many challenges, most of which will revolve around herding "the talent" toward new and unfamiliar ways of working. To change a legal team, you have to change the team members' behaviors, often moving people out of their comfort zones or away from the things they have always associated with defining their value. It's not easy for the leader or the team member.

Lawyers and professional staff on legal teams are what some refer to as "elevator assets" – when they get into the elevator after a day at the office, all of the value and capital associated with their work goes with them. So change leaders have to walk the fine line of pushing enough, but not too much. There will always be a segment of the team that embraces the opportunity to change as the best path to their future success, and will join in to do whatever is asked of them. There will be others who sit on the fence to wait and see if the change will be successful or beneficial before they'll commit, but they can be convinced. And unfortunately, there will always be some who simply won't change and will openly or through subterfuge work to scuttle progress. Eventually, the GC will need to decide if that kind of resistance will be tolerated, and it will be the true test of the department's commitment to driving change.

As a result, the work of change managers is a delicate balance between inspiration and leadership; therapy and stark realities. Change team leaders have to think not just about the projects and practices they want to implement, but how they can better engage and leverage the talent that will make them succeed or fail.

They will likely need to focus on:

- How to determine what each team member's highest contributions might be, and move them toward those tasks, rather than allowing them to wallow in lower value work that should be sent to others or outsourced or automated or eliminated;
- How to create a workplace culture that is inclusive and engages every team member, supporting of their wellbeing, work–life balance, and passions inside and outside of work;
- How to find and retain/hire the right talent for different and ever-emerging client needs;
- How to advance the careers of workers at all levels, offering them challenging roles and career paths, and educational enrichment to expand their value (even if it is not possible to offer unlimited opportunities for promotion);
- How to evaluate team member performance based on articulated goals and expectations, and then properly reward those who excel, and address, re-train, or eventually discipline/terminate those who aren't contributing as they should;
- How to prioritize and support collaborative relationships between lawyers and teams – inside and outside of the department; and

- How to value and recognize the contributions of lawyers, operations leaders, administrators, paraprofessionals and other experts, and encourage them to understand, respect, and leverage each other's expertise.

Once the team is moving toward new ways of working, the GC must decide on how to anoint and empower the person or team that will carry the ongoing responsibility for continuing the work of running an efficient and effective law department after the initial projects are on rails. When change initiatives appear novel and innovative, there is a level of excitement in joining the fray; over time, like everything, success will be determined by determination and the daily slog through the tasks necessary to drive the projects forward and institutionalize them, engage in continuous improvement, and report results. That kind of work is not possible to do part-time or without accountability and authority.

For an increasing number of departments and firms, the answer is the installation of a senior legal operations professional. Some GCs hire legal ops leaders to help develop and define the change initiative from the start, and others hire them after they have worked with the internal legal team to define what kinds of change they'd like to prioritize. Regardless of when the ops leader is brought on board, what is important is to vest in that person or team the kinds of responsibilities often associated with a chief of staff or CAO. Legal ops cannot be successful if it's relegated to a dark corner of the department, without empowering it with the expertise, authority, and budget to enlist and hold every legal team member accountable to the plan. Some ops leaders are lawyers, often from the department, but an increasing number do not have a law degree or even much previous experience with legal service provision – they bring the skills of other business disciplines since those are what counts most in driving better business practices. Many have MBAs in executive management, or significant experience in disciplines such as finance, digital transformation, information technology, and human resources.

An increasing number of organizations are focusing attention on the role and expertise of legal operations leaders, including CLOC (the Corporate Legal Operations Consortium),[1] ACC Legal Ops,[2] consulting firms, and local and international bar associations.

Final thoughts

While there are many approaches and opinions about these issues and I may be right or wrong, it's clear that the consequences of inaction or stalled progress toward change are significant and severe. I believe that many lawyers are on the road to irrelevance – and it's not because clients don't need lawyers or won't be paying for services that lawyers can provide. It's because some lawyers aren't willing to evaluate their practices and value through the lens of their clients. I predict that at some time in the near future, those who aren't on board the client train toward better practices are in danger of either being left standing on the platform as the train rolls by, or will be run over while wandering around on the tracks looking for work.

There is a greater than ever need for legal services and great lawyering, but a quickly growing frustration with the legal profession's inability to get out of its own way and fulfill burgeoning and emerging client needs and the public's expectation of more efficient and equitable systems for administering justice. The inevitable result is that clients of all kinds – from those who can't afford representation to those who can get what they want from other sources – will be far more likely to look for solutions to their problems that don't involve a lawyer at all. I couldn't blame them if they did, nor would I reproach the intelligent businesspeople who figured out how to beat us at our own game.

Law firms at the top of their game will continue to make terrific money and support many loyal corporate clients, but they will do so because clients have decided they want what they provide and not because there is no other alternative. Many of those firms will survive because they have shifted what they "sell" to what clients want to "buy", and not because they can unilaterally decide what they want to sell and how it's delivered. In-house counsel should pay heed as well, since they are currently only one step removed from their brethren in firms, and two steps closer to the corporate budget axe.

While the past is written, the continuing and future evolution of GCs and their legal teams is yet to be determined. I, for one, can't wait to see where it goes and am excited by the options we've yet to explore.

References

1 www.cloc.org
2 www.acc.com/legalops

Chapter 2:
The general counsel, corporate governance, and stakeholder capitalism

By Bruno Cova, partner, Delfino Willkie Farr & Gallagher, and Leanne Geale, executive vice president and general counsel, corporate governance and compliance, Nestlé S.A.

Introduction

In this chapter we will argue that what is already a key proving ground for general counsel,[1] corporate governance, is becoming even more relevant in the age of stakeholder capitalism. We will examine why this is the case and address some of the issues that are likely to become of greater relevance.

While the role of general counsel in ESG is specifically addressed in another chapter of this book,[2] the G in the acronym stands for Governance, and we will therefore be mindful of how the other two elements of the acronym, Environmental and Social, are intertwined with governance.

The views of the authors on the role and relevance of corporate governance for a general counsel are colored by their experiences and perspectives. One of the authors is a senior executive and general counsel at a global, listed company, having worked over 30 years at five listed multinationals in Canada and Europe across five industries. The other author is a private legal practitioner advising boards of directors and senior legal officers on corporate governance and legal and compliance risk issues, with a past as general counsel and director of listed and unlisted companies, and since 2012 serving[3] as advisor to the Corporate Governance Committee of companies listed on the Milan stock exchange.

The views expressed by the authors are personal and do not necessarily reflect the position of the organizations to which they belong.

Factors driving the role of general counsel in corporate governance

Over the centuries, more and more of the world's economic development, balance of power, scientific progress, and social welfare has come to depend on the success of corporations. Therefore, it is no surprise that society at large has a keen interest and stake in how corporations operate and are governed. Popular attention to corporate behavior has naturally increased in conjunction with the growth of companies and their power. In response, many companies are now actively embracing ESG and better governance, as well as helping to push the agenda more broadly.

Developments over the last 20 years have propelled the general counsel and her team to a prominent position in corporate governance, and the trend towards stakeholder capitalism (and the related focus on ESG) requires that the role of the general counsel in a company's governance be reconsidered and better defined.

We will first look at the trends of the last two decades and then to the challenges of stakeholder capitalism.

Growth of legal risk[4]

The rate of change in business has accelerated, thus creating a constant flow of previously unknown challenges. Globalization has multiplied the number and complexity (including inconsistencies) of applicable legal standards and the risk of multi-jurisdictional enforcement actions; at the same time regulatory and enforcement agencies have become more assertive, have often seen their powers and their resources enhanced, and are increasingly adept at dealing with complexities and cooperating across borders. The current (2022) partial retreat from globalization is posing its own challenges.

Further, so-called soft law is fast becoming hard law, more actors are using litigation with innovative theories of liability and funding mechanisms, and technology can enable and expose business practices. However, until confronted with the challenges these developments can bring, many companies have underappreciated the importance of a full understanding of applicable regulatory regimes, or the way courts of law operate, or even having adequate legal infrastructure (members of legal and compliance departments, trusted and competent outside counsel).

The increase in legal risks for the company has been accompanied by a similar trend for individuals so that directors and senior managers are and feel increasingly personally exposed to legal risk. Some regulators have made a point of focusing on holding individuals accountable.[5] As a result, interest in company indemnities and D&O insurance has increased, as has the cost of insurance coverage.

Increasingly pervasive regulation

Largely as a consequence of major governance failures, boards of directors are increasingly being asked – by statutes, by voluntary codes of corporate governance, or simply by market expectations – to identify, control, and manage risks, often with an emphasis on legal and compliance risk. Several countries have passed legislation[6] *de facto* mandating companies to introduce internal controls to prevent wrongdoing, sometimes to comply with international treaties or multilateral obligations (e.g., the 1997 OECD Convention on Combating Bribery of Foreign Officials or the reforms of banking law in the European Union). Some of the new rules attribute specific roles to lawyers in the prevention of wrongdoing (e.g., Section 307 of the US Sarbanes-Oxley Act; the tasks attributed by regulations to compliance officers in insurance companies, banks, and other financial institutions; anti-money laundering legislation).

Public and media attention regarding the the behavior of corporations has increased, and the effects of such attention have been enhanced by the growth and immediacy of social media. In the case of listed companies, disclosure obligations now encompass so-called non-financial information,[7] including information on how companies are managing compliance risks such as bribery and the results of whistleblower helplines. Further, plaintiffs lawyers, non-governmental organizations (NGOs) and activist investment funds are becoming increasingly adept at leveraging legal arguments and the courts of law to promote and further their agenda.[8]

These changes have produced an environment in which legal risk has arguably become one of the most important short-term risks for any company, which can transform the future of a corporation in a matter of days or weeks.

The combination of a failure of internal controls and legal or compliance risks can in fact:

- Bring a company to its dissolution, as was famously the case for auditing firm Arthur Andersen in the wake of the Enron debacle, and more recently for international supplier of electronic payment and risk management services Wirecard in Germany;
- Cause changes in ownership (e.g., at Parmalat, AIG, Citibank, Royal Bank of Scotland and various other banks during the financial crisis of 2008-2009) or senior management (e.g., at UBS, Marsh McLennan, Barclays Bank, Saipem, Siemens, and Volkswagen); and
- Produce changes in strategy, such as the shedding or dramatic downsizing of the investment banking business at several international banks following the 2008 financial crisis.

Often, legal (including regulatory) risks are a consequence and can become a multiplier of other risks, such as accounting (at Enron, Parmalat and Monte dei Paschi di Siena); product liability (at Ford and Firestone, Volkswagen, and General Motors); environmental (at BP in connection with the 2010 Deep Horizon oil spill in the Gulf of Mexico, and at Volkswagen following the emission scandal); and protection of personal data (at News Corporation, Deutsche Telekom, and Telecom Italia).

Corporate interest and stakeholder capitalism

In many circumstances, identifying what – in a specific case – is in the best interest of a company is not an easy exercise. With the emergence of stakeholder capitalism, things have become a bit more complicated. What was already often a very difficult assessment is becoming increasingly complex due to the moving and often highly disputed definition of corporate interest.

The corporate interest or interest of the company standard is a longstanding basic legal construct. It requires that actions by directors on behalf of a company have reasonably positive consequences for the company. The standard is intended to protect shareholders from abuses of power by those directing the company, that is a situation in which a few individuals have access to and can dispose of shareholders' money.

The violation of the corporate interest standard is typically sanctioned by criminal or financial liability for directors or may result in the voiding of the transaction. Various legal systems also adopt corporate governance measures to reduce the risk of violations of the corporate interest standard, such as obligations to disclose a personal interest in a transaction, safeguards for transactions with related parties, the presence of a minimum number of independent board members, and the criteria to determine their independence.

Since the 1970s, the prevailing interpretation of corporate interest has been driven by Milton Friedman's "shareholder primacy" doctrine whereby shareholder interest should have priority to that of other corporate stakeholders.[9]

The financial crisis of 2008 marked the beginning of soul-searching regarding the shareholder primacy doctrine, a process that in 2019 famously led to the Business Roundtable publishing its statement[10] redefining the purpose of a corporation "*to benefit all stakeholders – customers, employees, suppliers, communities and shareholders*". Since then, the increasing acknowledgment and understanding of the risks associated with climate change and the effects of the COVID-19 pandemic have created additional momentum for the principle of stakeholder capitalism.

Employees, consumers, investors, the general public, and others have been instrumental in inspiring the demand that corporations aim at more than just profit maximization.

This movement is encouraged by state interventionism, which operates through a mixture of international legal instruments (such as the EU rules on non-financial disclosure, sustainability-related disclosures in the financial services sector, and the framework to facilitate sustainable investment), domestic statutes (such as Germany's Supply Chain Due Diligence Act of 2021, the French Due Diligence Law of 2017, or the laws encouraging so-called benefit corporations in various North American, South American, and European countries), as well as consumer decision-making and moral suasion.

Some corporations (particularly listed ones, often encouraged to do so by legislation, voluntary codes of corporate governance, and investors) have defined what they believe is their corporate interest. The majority of companies have not and will not. A general counsel, when asked to assess whether a particular action meets the corporate interest standard, may therefore have the ability to refer to how the company's board of directors defined the company's corporate interest, or not. In all cases, shareholders may disagree with the directors' interpretation of corporate interest and the ultimate arbiter of whether an action meets the corporate interest standard may well be a court of law.

Ensuring general counsel's effective corporate governance role

To assess the role of a general counsel in corporate governance, one must start with a thorough understanding of the responsibilities of those bodies that, under company law, govern the corporation on behalf of its shareholders.

A corporation's governance structure can vary depending on:

- The governance systems required or permitted by local legislation (e.g., one-tier and two-tier boards, or the presence of a board of statutory auditors);
- The type of company (e.g., Ltd or Plc);
- Whether the company is private or has its shares or other financial instruments listed on a stock exchange;
- The preferences of the shareholders; and
- Whether the entity operates in a regulated market (e.g., in the banking, insurance, or financial sectors).

To avoid being dispersive in looking at all the various options, this chapter will generally consider a listed company with a one-tier board of directors, with part of its members sitting on various committees, including an audit committee tasked with supervising the company's internal controls and risk management system. We will also assume that the general counsel acts as secretary of the board of directors and leads the corporate secretariat function of the company.

While directors' duties can vary from one jurisdiction to another, they generally encompass providing strategic direction and acting in the company's corporate interest. As part of this, directors must focus on ensuring that the company operates in compliance with applicable laws and its by-laws, and properly addresses legal risks.

Therefore, the board has a keen interest in ensuring the effectiveness of the various corporate functions – in particular, those that have a role in ensuring effective risk management and internal controls, such as the audit, risk control, legal, and compliance functions.

The ability of a general counsel to contribute to governance issues depends on a number of factors, starting with the personal skills of the individual, but also including whether the general counsel is put in a position to make that contribution. Some of these factors are described below. The responsibility for ensuring that a general counsel is well placed to contribute on governance issues lies with the board of directors and the company's management.

The board's interest in ensuring that it can benefit from the general counsel's contribution must lead it to address the role of the general counsel and the legal function within the company as a whole. Failing to address the role of the general counsel can lead to dire consequences for the company.[11]

Reporting lines

Ideally, the general counsel should directly report to the company's CEO, as this will ensure that the general counsel has a direct line to the company's leader and is perceived within the corporation as an influential executive who is a member of the company's top management. Reporting to the CEO also sends a clear signal inside and outside the company that abiding by the law, strong enforcement of the company's legal and contractual rights, and legal risk management are important features of the company's attitude to doing business.

Other reporting lines (e.g., to the chief operating officer (COO) or the CFO, or even to the chief human resources officer) are possible, but clearly not ideal in terms of corporate governance. A board should be skeptical of such arrangements and satisfy itself that they do not interfere with a general counsel's ability to do her job in a way that is consistent with the company's objectives and internal control requirements.

When the general counsel is also company secretary, it is not uncommon for her to report to the company's chair, or to have a dual reporting to the chair as company secretary, and to the CEO as general counsel.

In some corporations the general counsel reports directly to the board. This solution emphasizes the general counsel's independence from management and stresses her role as part of the company's internal control system but is often impractical and diminishes a general counsel's ability to be perceived as a member of the company's executive team. The general counsel does, however, need to have open communications with the board and its committees, but this can be achieved outside a direct reporting arrangement.

Reporting lines are as important between the general counsel of the parent company and the heads of legal services in its subsidiaries as they are between the general counsel and the CEO and the board. In fact, it is often the case that legal risks originate in a subsidiary, not at parent company level.[12]

All heads of legal services in the company's subsidiaries should therefore report to the general counsel – either directly or through other members of the legal function. If the reporting is only functional (in corporate jargon, dotted line), then it should consist of at least three elements:

- The head of legal cannot be appointed or removed without the general counsel's consent;
- His or her fixed and variable salary should be determined by or in consultation with the general counsel; and
- The budget and resources of the subsidiary's legal department should be determined in consultation with the general counsel.

The general counsel would thus have the "carrots and sticks" to ensure the subsidiary's head of legal's independence from local management and loyalty to the corporation as a whole, not to the local operating company or local CEO.

Sitting on the board

Some general counsel are members of their company's board. This is clearly a negative in terms of corporate governance, as it makes the general counsel her own client and blurs the lines of what should be the clearly defined tasks of a general counsel.

However, the general counsel could take a directorship in a subsidiary. This can greatly help a general counsel to understand the dynamics of a board of directors. However, a directorship in a subsidiary may lead to awkward conflict of interest situations, for instance when the parent company is in financial distress and is trying to obtain financial resources from its subsidiaries; when the subsidiary becomes involved in wrongdoing; or when there is tension between a general counsel's confidentiality obligations to the parent company and her duty as a director to report information of material importance to the subsidiary. The problem is obviously compounded if there are other shareholders in the subsidiary.

One salary, but many roles

The three most senior legal or quasi-legal roles in a corporation are those of general counsel, company secretary, and chief compliance officer. Each corporation has its own recipe for whether these roles should all be covered by one individual or by separate individuals, or combined in pairs, or covered by different individuals reporting to a chief legal officer. This disparity of views is quite appropriate given the different requirements of each corporation, which may vary over the years.

Certain regulators have taken the view that the chief compliance officer should not be the general counsel or report to her. In deciding whether a general counsel should also be given the role of company secretary and/or chief compliance officer, in addition to giving due consideration to any industry sector regulation, the board should carefully assess whether a multiplicity of roles might hinder the individual's ability to act with a sufficient degree of independence in each role. In the event that the three roles are kept separate with no reporting lines between them, the board should satisfy itself that adequate cooperation protocols exist to allow each officer to benefit from the others' input when relevant.

Attending board meetings

Even when the general counsel is not the secretary of the board, she should be invited to attend all board meetings, as well as the meetings of certain board committees, such as the audit and risk committees. Such participation is necessary to ensure that the general counsel is aware of any issue discussed by the board that may have an impact on the company's legal risk. The general counsel's presence will also allow the board to seek her view on any corporate governance or legal risk issue.

In the same vein, the board should verify whether the general counsel or a member of the legal department should be given the opportunity to sit on those company's internal committees where legal risk issues may arise, such as the executive committee, investment committee, risk committee, disclosure committee, or sustainability committee.

Access to adequate resources

The growing demands on legal departments are often at odds with an overall reduction in the resources made available to them, often resulting in increased exposure to legal risks that cannot be adequately managed. The board should assess whether the legal and compliance functions have an adequate level of resources to fulfil the tasks attributed to them in the context of the external regulatory environment applicable to the corporation and the internal controls and risk management system of the corporation.

Outside counsel

Most corporations source their legal requirements through a combination of internal and external legal services. The general counsel should have ultimate responsibility for all legal matters, including those handled by outside counsel, which are an integral part of the company's legal risk management system. The board should ensure that the general counsel (and not other officers, such as the CFO) is responsible for the selection and management of outside counsel.

This approach is also beneficial to outside counsel, who will deal with a company officer who is ideally suited to providing clear instructions and all necessary information, and who can ensure that external advice is appropriately disseminated within the company and its functions.

Choice of general counsel and control of financial incentives

Considering the importance of corporate governance and legal risk to a corporation, directors should take an interest in who the general counsel is and the way in which her performance is rewarded and incentivized.

Directors are generally involved in the selection of the head of the internal audit function (in certain regulated industries, also of other executive roles such as the chief compliance officer and the chief risk officer) and they should be involved in the choice of the company's general counsel. As a matter of fact, choosing the right general counsel is usually more complex than choosing the internal auditor, because the corporate governance and legal risk profile of a company can change considerably over the years. For example, years ago the vast majority of general counsel had a transactional background, while these days, litigation or regulatory experience have become far more relevant.

To avoid the risk of perverse incentives, a general counsel's compensation and the criteria for determining its variable elements should be set by or in consultation with the board of directors or a board committee.

A board of directors' interest in the general counsel should also extend to her removal. Directors should make clear to management that they will interview a general counsel if she is removed or leaves the company for no obvious reasons, or if her responsibilities are changed.

The Mad Hatter – coping with unique and multiple roles

The general counsel often wears many hats. She provides legal advice to the board of directors and senior management, and – through the legal department – advises senior and mid-level management; leads and administers the legal department; is a member of the company's senior executive team; and procures and manages outside legal services.

Often, the general counsel is also the company secretary and occasionally the chief compliance officer. In some cases, she is also given additional responsibilities, such as administering the company's real estate or IP assets, or leading the tax, procurement, government relations, communications, or security functions.

While all general counsel and legal functions play a role in corporate governance, the boundaries of the role change from one organization to another, as well as over the years. There is no one recipe that works for all companies or for the same company at all times. The reason is clear – companies are different and change over time. For instance, the corporate governance role of the legal department in a listed and/or regulated company will be different from that in a portfolio company of a private equity fund or a family-owned company, and its involvement in corporate governance issues will change considerably depending on whether the situation is a proxy fight or takeover battle, or a regulatory investigation.

As a senior officer of her company, the general counsel has a broad range of relationships with parties inside and outside the company. Some of these relationships are clear and no different from those of a similarly senior officer – for example, the general counsel is the leader of her team; a colleague and a peer of other senior managers; a service provider to senior management; the client of external providers of legal and other services.

However, other relationships are unique to the role of general counsel. She is probably one of only a handful of senior company officers with direct access to the board (the others usually being the CFO and the head of internal audit). Even so, although the roles of the CFO and the head of internal audit (of listed companies) are regulated in many countries, the general counsel's role in relation to the board, the company, or the markets is typically not regulated by the law, the company's by-laws or voluntary codes of corporate governance (other than – and to a limited extent – in connection with the general counsel's tasks as company secretary). The interaction between the general counsel, the board, the company, and the markets is largely left to each company's own internal regulation.

However, in some jurisdictions, the general counsel does have certain specific legal obligations, such as under rules attributing specific roles to lawyers in the prevention of wrongdoing (e.g., Section 307 of the US Sarbanes-Oxley Act), or may have their role as chief compliance officer defined by industry regulators (e.g., in the banking sector).

By the nature of her role (and in some cases to abide by applicable codes of conduct for members of the bar or of the in-house profession), the general counsel must act in what is in her own interpretation the best interest of the corporation, rather than in what the CEO or even the board believes is its best interest. This issue becomes particularly acute when there is the possibility of conflicts of interest or wrongdoing having occurred or potentially occurring.

General counsel increasingly play a major role in the corporate governance of their companies. What kind of corporate governance role is attributed to them is defined by a number of company-specific factors:

- The applicable legal regime (e.g., whether the company is listed or operates in a regulated sector and the extent to which local law regulates the role of the general counsel, the chief compliance officer, or the company secretary);
- Organizational issues (e.g., the attributions of the legal department and its organization; whether the compliance function is part of the legal department or a separate unit; the internal reporting lines; and whether the general counsel also acts as company secretary);
- Soft issues (e.g., the attitude of the CEO and chair to legal matters, the personality and credibility of the general counsel, and the attention paid by the board of directors to governance issues); and
- Factual circumstances (e.g., the ownership structure of the company or the presence of activist shareholders).

Therefore, the actual responsibilities of a general counsel and the legal department in the context of a company's corporate governance can vary considerably. Some of these responsibilities are outlined below.

Designing internal controls and risk management tools

The general counsel assists senior management and the board of directors in the design and adoption of the corporation's internal control and risk management system. Directors have an obligation (usually directly or indirectly enshrined in law and/or mandated by applicable codes of corporate governance or listing rules) to act in an informed manner and protect the company's interests. The internal control and risk management system is the organizational tool usually adopted to achieve the desired result. Legal departments play a key role in supporting senior management in designing such a system, usually taking primary responsibility for the development and implementation of policies to protect the company's assets (e.g., its intellectual property, its contractual rights and the operation of its procurement function) and to ensure compliance with the law (e.g., in the areas of antitrust, bribery, transactions with related parties, market abuse, money laundering, and the protection of whistleblowers). Moreover, legal departments often support other corporate functions in the development and implementation of additional relevant policies (e.g., on disclosure or financial reporting).

Given the trend towards stakeholder capitalism and the increased importance of ESG issues, the general counsel must have a key role in ensuring that those elements are also factored into the company's policies. In this way the policies will be effective tools not only to ensure that the company abides by the law, but also addresses ESG risks.

Legal risk assessment

The focus on risks has become an integral part of many corporate governance systems and – as stated above – legal risks are among the main risks faced by corporations. The general counsel and the legal department usually assist senior management and the board of directors in their assessment of legal risks or support – where present – the risk function in assessing legal risks. A legal department will typically be involved in the mapping and measurement of legal risks, whether as part of a periodic risk assessment or within the context of specific transactions (e.g., a joint venture or the acquisition of assets or other companies) or developments in the company's strategy (e.g., entry in new markets).

The assessment of legal risk must go hand-in-hand with the assessment of any ESG risk that may be associated with a particular transaction, litigation, or enforcement action. Particular attention should be paid to the interconnection between ESG and legal risks, as for instance in evaluating the possibility of an NGO using the law and the judicial system to promote its agenda. As legal and non-legal risks converge, the general counsel is in a unique position to take a holistic view of a situation and "connect the dots" between risks, thereby enabling a more robust action plan or response.

Advice on corporate governance matters

The general counsel advises senior management and the board of directors on specific corporate governance issues, ranging from routine matters (the evaluation of the independence of directors or related party transactions) to extraordinary circumstances (a hostile takeover of the company) and major crises (criminal or regulatory investigations). The latter are areas in which the general counsel is often put to the test, as we will see later.

Ensuring the functioning of the board and its committees

When the general counsel is also the company secretary, she will be responsible for the minutes of board of directors' meetings and will generally assist the company's chair in managing her responsibilities – such as convening board meetings or providing timely information to the directors. Likewise, the general counsel as secretary will often be given the responsibility of supporting the activities of certain committees of the board. In connection with these duties the general counsel can play a very useful role in ensuring the effective functioning of the board of directors and resolving occasional conflicts that may arise.

Dealing with regulators

In listed companies, the general counsel is often the primary liaison between the company and the stock exchange regulator. She often has primary responsibility for the interaction with other regulators, such as antitrust authorities or industry supervisors (e.g., in the banking and insurance sectors), or in the event of an external investigation. It is not unusual for the general counsel also to play a role in the corporation's advocacy efforts in relation to future legislation and regulation – either directly or through industry associations.

Role model of company values

The general counsel should also be a visible and vocal model of the corporation's core values. If the company's senior-most legal and compliance officer doesn't defend, uphold, and live the company's values, it makes it difficult to hold the rest of the organization to account. This can often play out in the "gray areas" of legality and heavily influence the actions of a corporation.

In addition to advising on whether or not something is legal or compliant, the general counsel is often in a position to advise on consistency of positions and actions taken that can positively or negatively impact the company's reputation and its credibility vis-à-vis multiple stakeholders.

This is even more true as stakeholder capitalism and external scrutiny grows.

Corporate governance issues for general counsel

The legal department's involvement in corporate governance can have a significant impact on how a corporate (in-house) counsel's performance is viewed by the company. For example, they can demonstrate their ability to enable the company's business strategy by advising on legal risk and raise senior management's awareness of the many ways that the legal function contributes value to the company. At the same time, the legal function's involvement in governance helps the company to ensure that it has effective internal controls and a correct assessment of legal risks, enabling its board of directors to function well and fulfil its duties.

The majority of a general counsel's corporate governance responsibilities are discharged as routine matters that usually do not pose particular challenges to a well-qualified professional and her team. Given the importance of a general counsel's contribution to corporate governance in particularly demanding situations, we will turn to certain specific challenges that a company lawyer may face.

Addressing and solving conflicts on the board

The board is, by definition, a difficult constituency to deal with. It is there to support the CEO, but also to ensure the affairs of the company are being properly managed. It can consist of people with different interpretations of their role or with different agendas (e.g., directors elected by activist shareholders).[13] It is invariably made up of clever people with strong personalities. The general counsel (particularly when wearing the hat of company secretary) can and often does play a useful role in the resolution of conflicts arising on the board.

Her role in these circumstances is primarily to ensure that the law and the company's code of conduct and governance rules are observed, and that the company accurately reports what must be reported to the markets and the regulators. Often, her role is extended to dissecting disputed matters and providing advice on how to resolve a dispute.

When a conflict arises between the CEO (usually the general counsel's boss) and the board, the situation is particularly complex. Some of these conflicts may occur because the board is dissatisfied with the CEO's strategy or work, or because of inadequate communication or lack of trust. Other – and more complex from a general counsel's perspective – conflicts may occur because of possible violations of the CEO's duties (e.g., violations of the law, the company's by-laws or its policies; the CEO's failure to report fully to the board; or the CEO's disregard for the board's instructions). These situations test a general counsel's ability to be an effective custodian of the legality of the company's actions, as well as an agent the board can rely on to ensure effective corporate governance. A general counsel's ability to deal effectively with these situations will depend on a combination of professional skills and courage, the quality of the board, and on the mechanics of the company's governance. As discussed earlier in this chapter, it is up to the board to ensure that the general counsel is put in the position when necessary to stand up effectively to the CEO and other senior managers and adopt the necessary measures.

Counselling individual board members

Directors are often concerned about their personal liability. In the United States, long-serving directors of listed companies can almost take it for granted that sooner or later they will be subject to legal action by an aggressive plaintiff. Personal legal exposure has also become more common in other jurisdictions.

Particularly when investigations are of a criminal nature, even the potential for personal liability is extremely upsetting to board members because of the associated negative publicity which – in addition to soiling a reputation they have built over often remarkable careers – can hinder their ability to serve in other capacities.

Directors concerned about their personal position will be tempted to turn to the general counsel for advice. Counselling them creates a conflict of interest for the general counsel, who should therefore avoid providing personal legal advice to directors. If the issue of concern is company-related, the company could always make outside counsel available to the relevant director.

Reacting to disclosure of confidential information

Another difficult situation for a general counsel is when there is suspicion that one or more directors or peer senior managers are leaking confidential information to the press or other parties, such as competitors or companies attempting to take over the corporation.

Leaking information is clearly a violation of a director's or senior manager's duty of confidentiality to the company and may amount to market abuse or insider trading. The general counsel will have played a role in devising company policies aimed at ensuring the confidentiality of the information made available to the board and the management committee and will have to assess whether further measures are warranted in the circumstances. She will also have to advise on what steps should be taken to identify the culprit – either through internal investigations or by seeking the cooperation of the relevant public authorities – and on what measures should be taken when the source of the leak is identified.

Assessing her own independence

Particularly in the context of corporate governance, a general counsel is expected to act with independence. The authors believe that in-house counsel lawyers are not less independent per se than outside counsel, and independence should be tested in relation to a particular set of circumstances. In our opinion there are plenty (actually, the majority) of situations where a general counsel will be more independent than a private practitioner, and others where only the latter will be the sufficiently independent resource available to the company.

The following factors can compromise the independence of general counsel:

- The employment relationship with a single client, which calls into question the feasibility of withdrawing from representation if professional rules so require;
- The fact that general counsel are usually members of the senior management team, which creates bonds of personal loyalty; and
- The inherent conflict that a general counsel may face when called to question matters on which she has advised.

Private practitioners are not strangers to these factors. They may be fearful of losing an important client; they have long-term relationships with, and may be loyal to, certain members of the company's management team; and they may be reluctant to revisit positions on which they have advised. However, the same factors that are considered to raise questions about a general counsel's independence may also constitute an advantage. It can be argued that a general counsel's knowledge of the company, its management and the situation at hand, as well as her commitment to the company, can make the company lawyer the best resource for independently assessing the relevant corporate governance issue.

In our view, the concept of independence varies, usually depending on facts related to the specific issue to be addressed. The company lawyer's independence may need to be evaluated in relation to the following:

- A shareholder or group of shareholders (e.g., in the context of related party transactions or proxy fights);
- The CEO or other senior managers (e.g., if wrongdoing is alleged against the CEO or a senior manager); or
- The lawyer herself (e.g., a matter in which the lawyer's past advice is questioned).

General counsel should objectively evaluate whether they are sufficiently independent to address a specific corporate governance issue and, when in doubt, seek outside advice or openly discuss the issue with the board or the audit committee. In doing so, general counsel should consider the issues' possible future ramifications, to ensure that their independence will survive the test of expected future developments.

Exercising great caution in the context of internal investigations

The biggest test of a general counsel's independence is often an internal investigation – particularly when it deals with alleged wrongdoing by the CEO or senior managers within the context of criminal or regulatory investigations. Such investigations are a common graveyard for legal and managerial careers.

These situations demonstrate the friction between being a member of the senior management team and a loyal professional friend of the CEO and other senior managers, and the duties of the general counsel to the corporation. Mistakes are easily made and can have dire consequences for the company and the general counsel's own credibility. The most common mistake is that of confusing one's duty to the corporation with one's loyalty to the CEO and the senior management team.

In these circumstances, the board and the general counsel should each take steps to ensure the independence of the investigation.

The board should carefully scrutinize the way in which the investigation is conducted and take the appropriate corporate governance measures to ensure that it receives an unadulterated flow of information, the investigation and the defense of the company are not conducted in a manner that is inappropriately influenced by the CEO, and disclosure by the company is coherent with the facts. In many cases this can involve the board itself, or a committee of the board, taking direct responsibility for the investigation – often hiring an independent outside counsel.

The general counsel should carefully reflect on her responsibilities to the company and define an action plan that satisfies the independence requirements of effective corporate governance. This can involve painful choices, such as delegating the investigation work to an independent outside counsel; having the board of directors appoint an independent legal advisor; or "shutting out" the CEO or the relevant senior managers from information on the investigation.

Failure to govern the investigation properly or allowing the CEO or senior managers to influence the investigation, the company's defense strategy and/or disclosure can have unpleasant consequences for the company. The board and the general counsel may be accused of allowing or enabling tampering with evidence, obstructing the course of justice, or providing misleading disclosure to the markets or regulators.

Being honest about one's own conflicts of interest

Whether in the context of regulatory investigations or otherwise, the general counsel may be asked to review transactions on which she advised. Her independence may be viewed as compromised when reviewing her own work or the work of her legal department.

In this case, the general counsel should take all appropriate measures to ensure that the review can be conducted without being improperly influenced. These measures will typically involve having the review conducted by company lawyers (or outside counsel) who were not involved in advising on the original transaction.

With a view to ensuring its own ability to act on the basis of independent advice, the board should be mindful of the risks associated with these kinds of conflict of interest and satisfy itself that the measures adopted are adequate.

Dealing with other lawyers on the board

Given the growing risks associated with regulatory and legal matters, there is a trend of appointing lawyers to the board. The presence of other lawyers on the board can be helpful or harmful, depending on the lawyer-director.

Their legal background can be valuable to the company in understanding, explaining, and supporting advice or legal strategies from the general counsel. The lawyer-director can also provide additional perspectives to the matter, based on their experience. However, they should be careful not to interfere with the general counsel, let alone provide legal advice to the board. If the lawyer-director is a non-independent member of the board, there is also the risk of him being or trying to become an outside counsel to the company, which would put the general counsel in a difficult situation.

The general counsel should openly discuss the situation with the lawyer-director and, if necessary, enlist the chair's or the CEO's support in dealing with the circumstance, with a view to ensuring that there is no confusion of roles.

Corporate governance involves personal risks and opportunities

A normal state of affairs is a temporary condition for most corporations. With ever-increasing frequency, unexpected events call a company's corporate governance into question. These events can include a dispute between shareholders or at board level, a proxy fight, a change of control, a major transaction, a reputational crisis, or a criminal or regulatory investigation. In these situations, the career of the general counsel can be made or destroyed, and she is put to a major test.

There are plenty of excellent articles describing the skills that a company lawyer should have to handle these situations and providing advice to general counsel. These articles are usually written by, or based on stories of, general counsel who got it right, and they provide useful suggestions. Other enlightening articles could be written by those general counsel who got it wrong. Not surprisingly, failure is not advertised by its protagonists and the literature of blunders is often written in the form of criminal indictments or enforcement actions.

The importance of legal issues has simultaneously enhanced the role of the legal function and created greater risks for company lawyers – occasionally taking the form of criminal or other enforcement action. A phenomenon traditionally associated with the United States, it has spread to Europe and beyond.

From a corporate governance standpoint, a general counsel's role is beneficial not only to her company, but also indirectly to society, by helping to steer the policies of the corporation and its reactions in socially desirable directions – that is, in directions that maximize the business' chances of success, protect the company's assets, enhance the reputation of the corporation, adhere to business principles, and generally help the corporation act as a "good citizen".

In the current environment of increasing legal risks, heightened enforcement, and stakeholder capitalism, a company lawyer's active role in corporate governance can often result in her biggest contribution to the corporation's wellbeing and to society in general, as no one else within a corporation is as well-equipped as a general counsel to support the board and senior management on governance matters.

References

1 Throughout this chapter, references to "general counsel" and "the legal function" should be read as references also to the chief compliance officer and the compliance function, and to the corporate secretary and her team. The issue of disparate legal roles within a corporation will be addressed in "The Mad Hatter" section.

2 See chapter ten.

3 Together with professors Piergaetano Marchetti and Angelo Provasoli of Bocconi University.

4 In this chapter, legal risk includes compliance risk unless otherwise indicated.

5 For example, see the reinstated Yates Memo from the US Department of Justice.

6 Such as the UK Bribery Act, Decree 231/2001 on the criminal liability of corporations in Italy, Loi Sapin II in France.

7 ESG non-financial disclosure is covered in chapter ten.

8 A notable case is the claim brought by Milieudefensie (Friends of the Earth Netherlands) and six other Dutch NGOs alongside c. 17,000 individual co-claimants before The Hague District Court, where the plaintiff was funded through crowd-funding. In its 2021 judgment, the court ordered Royal Dutch Shell plc to reduce its worldwide CO2 emissions by 45 percent by 2030 (compared to 2019 levels).

9 www.nytimes.com/1970/09/13/archives/a-friedman-doctrine-the-social-responsibility-of-business-is-to.html

10 https://s3.amazonaws.com/brt.org/BRT-StatementonthePurposeofaCorporationJuly2021.pdf

11 In 2004-2005 when one of the authors was chief legal advisor to the commissioner appointed by the Italian government to investigate Europe's largest financial fraud at Parmalat and restructure the company, as a former general counsel he studied with interest the reasons why such a large-scale fraud could be perpetrated over a period of 15 years without the company's legal department taking any action to prevent or stop it. In the author's conclusion, the reasons were as follows:

- The listed parent company did not have a legal department, as all the company lawyers were in the operating companies;
- The main operating company's general counsel reported to the chief financial

officer (CFO) and had no contact with the board of directors or the board of statutory auditors (a body with duties similar to those of an audit committee) or the external auditors of the company or its parent;

- The various legal departments in the foreign operating companies did not report to the main operating company's general counsel but to the local CEO or CFO;
- The general counsel had no control over outside legal spending – and 100 percent of the fraudulent transactions were in fact performed with the (generally unwitting) assistance of outside lawyers under the direction of the Chairman and CEO and the CFO; and
- The general counsel had no international experience, while nearly all the fraudulent transactions were conducted outside of Italy and were governed by laws other than the laws of Italy.

Parmalat's board of directors was clearly oblivious to the need to enlist the legal department as an agent of good corporate governance.

12 Using again Parmalat as an example, practically all the fraudulent transactions occurred at the level of the company's subsidiaries. This is consistent with the experience of countless other cases, where wrongdoing is almost invariably found to have been generated in or involved a subsidiary, often based in a foreign jurisdiction.

13 For example, the election of three directors on the ExxonMobil board following successful activism by Engine No. 1 in 2021.

Chapter 3:

The general counsel's role in the digital transformation of legal

By William L. Deckelman, Jr, executive vice president and general counsel, DXC Technology Company, and Daniel Reed, CEO, UnitedLex

When invited to write this chapter, we gave some thought to what would be most useful and valuable to in-house legal leaders at varying stages of digital transformation – including those who have not yet started! A fascinating part of digital transformation is that many aspects of it cannot be planned. As we progress, we make ongoing decisions and take on new aspects that become an integral part of the transformation. This is partly due to the changing business world and technology developments. Our digital focus must adapt to a full range of economic environments, not to mention our people's experience with using digital tools in their everyday work.

This helps to explain why digital transformation is never really finished. It is an ongoing evolution, as new digital tools are created and the organization's experience and situation lead us to identify new needs. We worked closely together from 2017 to 2022 on the digital transformation of DXC Technology's legal department. DXC Legal is well past Digital 101. After the initial test of proving the benefit of the organization's investments in digital, convincing business colleagues of the value was rarely an issue. But learning is continual. Any organization aiming to transform digitally will always be changing. It's essential to both celebrate great successes and decide on course corrections when an approach is no longer right for the moment.

This chapter focuses on these fundamental questions:

- Why should you as general counsel embrace digital transformation and convince your team to embrace it?
- What does it actually mean to be a digital legal department?
- Why do purpose and people come first in digital transformation?
- How does one address the massive topics of technology and data?

- What has worked in measuring value and showing we are meeting delivery goals?
- What are the key elements of digital transformation that every general counsel should remember?

There is no one way for a legal department to progress with digital transformation, just as there is no one type of company legal department. Every department, like every company, differs in significant ways.

Why should the general counsel and legal team embrace digital transformation?

Technology has changed the world significantly in the last decade, and the pace of change shows no signs of slowing. The global COVID-19 pandemic was an accelerator. Many companies are undergoing a systemic overhaul and fundamental shift in their priorities, relationships, operating models, and systems. They are pursuing a more impactful and stakeholder-centric operating model. If we look back at research over nearly a decade, CEOs have been increasingly certain that the digital trend would completely re-shape (and often disrupt) what they do and how they do it.

> *"Today, no company can make, deliver or market its product efficiently without technology."*[1]

No one would argue with this comment, but the legal sector has been slow to realize that the change also applies to it. In-house lawyers have often persisted with their traditional way of working as if they are different from the way their businesses operate. That is finally starting to change.

Today, digital transformation is a fundamental business objective and a strategic priority for all leading corporations across all sectors. Functions including legal, compliance, finance, Human Resources, and the supply chain are expected to adopt digital and be part of that transformation. Many general counsel have now recognized the need to advance through technology but lack confidence that they have the knowledge and skills to manage it.

A 2021 cross-industry study undertaken by the Economist Intelligence Unit, sponsored by Microsoft, polled 800 senior executives across eight sectors and 15 economies. A huge 72 percent of respondents to the survey reported a significant increase in investment in digital in their industry as a result of the pandemic.[2]

Successful business transformation demands enterprise-wide commitment. It requires collaboration across all teams and business units and alignment of the total workforce with a common goal. The legal department is no exception, not only to deliver advice that is relevant to new digital products and ways of thinking, but to improve the legal function's overall capability and do so far more efficiently.

Most businesses recognize that the legal function must be a part of the change process, though they may pay less attention to it than to their core lines of business. The C-suite is pressuring corporate legal leadership to deliver more and have a greater impact, to create enterprise value – in terms of revenue, cost, and risk – and to improve the overall end-user experience. Providing quality and efficient legal advice are table stakes, a hygiene factor in today's corporate landscape.

What happens if legal fails to make this change? In an enterprise-wide collaboration, there can be no weak links. If legal is the digital "laggard" in the transformation process, it will become disconnected from the business – its customer – and can no longer add value to the overall mission. If the general counsel and the legal department is not proactive in joining the rest of the business transformation journey, it will simply be compelled to change rather than owning the change itself. Or, worse, lose its ability to make a real impact, and fall behind in other areas of risk management.

Studies by both Gartner and McKinsey consistently show not only that a digital legal department creates significantly greater value compared to non-digital counterparts, but it also amplifies the success of distinct other digital initiatives across the organization.[3]

What is a "digital" legal department?

There is a common misconception that a digital legal department equates to technology only, heavily characterized by its adoption of technology platforms and products. While technology is certainly a key ingredient in the transformation and an enabler of that process, it is only one aspect.

Being digital requires a workforce that is tech-enabled, data-driven, agile, collaborative, customer-focused, multidisciplinary, cross-functional, diverse, possessing the required skills, and integrated.

A digital legal department is one that has completely reimagined how it operates and is undergoing a continuous, holistic program of change, in a way that is fully integrated with the business and focused on delivering a tangible positive impact and value.

Digital transformation is the integration of digital process and approach into all aspects of the production and delivery of legal services. It's also a cultural change that requires organizations to continually challenge the status quo, experiment with new ideas, and get comfortable with failure.

Value can be delivered in a variety of ways, both directly and indirectly. We can split these informally into Level One and Level Two organizational maturity. Level One maturity comprises all the things that many would refer to today as "legal operations", targeting efficiencies and cost savings, laying the foundations of change, and often leveraging legal tech point solutions. These aspects are essential, yet full transformation is unlikely to be achieved this way as it is a fairly slow and step-by-step process.

In Level One there are usually budgetary limitations to what is approved and what can be delivered. Level One almost never provides adequate advances for the legal function to show that it can simultaneously reduce costs, improve quality, and deliver tangible business value.

Delivering results that have a meaningful impact on the business can only be maximized through Level Two maturity. This requires a holistic change program – a literal re-thinking of the legal department, involving a broad and sweeping series of changes that enable the department to become data-driven.

How do you as general counsel achieve this? It starts and progresses with a vision – a "North Star" that defines and redefines the objectives of the digital journey and the results it expects to achieve. This requires changing how the legal department thinks and works. It necessitates a re-imagining of the traditional legal services model to make way for a more agile and customer-focused approach.

Why do purpose and people come first in digital transformation?

The legal department's vision and strategy must be clearly articulated and aligned to the goals and strategy of the wider organization. As a legal department leader, the general counsel must be able to help others visualize the benefits and the value they will bring. The general counsel must continually ensure that the team is committed and that every aspect of the digital transformation journey aligns with the purpose. The purpose of digital transformation pushes the legal department out of its silo and towards direct connections and participation with all other areas of the business.

Often this is easier for legal departments that have already developed strong business partnerships and the legal operations discipline; general counsel and their teams that have already worked to increase efficiency through different ways of working, including adopting new processes and new skills to gain productivity.

These legal departments will have been using metrics and be better able to find aspects of their function that can be made more efficient through changing structures, processes, or approaches. This experience is valuable because it provides proof of the benefits of digital progress and helps the team support and be enthusiastic about moving forward and embracing continual change.

At DXC Technology, the purpose of the corporate legal team from the start has been:

> *"To be the preeminent global innovator in digital transformation and world-class delivery of legal and commercial solutions to advance the mission of DXC Technology."*

That remains the vision.

For context, DXC Technology is a global IT and cloud services provider, born in 2017 out of a merger between a large part of Hewlett Packard Enterprise Services with Computer Sciences Corporation (CSC). The HPE and CSC merger provided a catalyst for the general counsel and team to embark on a digital transformation journey. The stages of that journey are outlined below.

The planning and execution of the vision started when the merger was announced. The merger would require the legal team to combine with another global legal contracting function, with the additional mandate that the total costs of the newly merged function must be cut by 30 percent in the first year. A daunting task for any corporate legal chief to face.

The combined leadership of the new DXC Legal determined that the only way it could achieve reduced costs of 30 percent in the first year, without drastically reducing its ability to deliver legal advice, would require a radical, disruptive change.

The DXC legal team recognized and was enthusiastic about the promises of digital. The horizon vision was that of a digitally-enhanced, data-driven, highly innovative organization that could lower costs significantly whilst providing significantly better legal and compliance support globally. A legal department that would be known for high performance that provided real value to the business and a healthy, fulfilling environment for our people.

At the outset, it was clear that new technology and process transformation was needed, and also evident that our culture – the way we interacted and approached our work – needed a reset. We did not recognize at the time how important both people and process would be to transformation.

A critical directive included moving DXC's legal department toward a more variable cost structure over the historical fixed-cost model. The goal was to provide enhanced scalability and resource flexibility for the department. This mandate required reimagining the traditional legal service delivery model.

The approach we took in 2017 may be very different than companies might take now. DXC Legal worked with UnitedLex and its captive law firm Marshall Denning to build a foundation to review and redesign the legal department's processes to simplify and enhance legal service delivery. The objective was to reduce compliance risk globally, and focus on people, including career development and mentoring. The three organizations collaborated in the important areas of training, professional development, and building a culture of agility, resilience, and innovation at all levels of the organization.

How does one address the massive topics of technology and data?

Technology is of course a central component of any digital transformation, and in DXC Legal's experience, we recognized a connected triangle as our key enabler – the interaction of people and processes with technology.

The primary objective of technology should always be to increase core efficiency and utility and demonstrate value recognized by the business. The aim is to facilitate better integration with the enterprise. The information and advice that comes from legal can thus be more useful to key business processes – for functions from compliance to product development and finance to sales.

It is rarely the "shiniest" new tech tools that help to achieve this. Often, focusing on the bread-and-butter applications and processes yield significant results without much additional cost.

To digitally transform, we found it necessary to access a robust productivity platform (think ERP for legal) that could provide transparency across the spectrum of legal work performed by internal and external resources. This new platform combined legal data with business data as a foundation for many digital applications, including some early experiments with Artificial Intelligence (AI).

The most immediate needs of the department focused around commercial contracting, which accounted for over 75 percent of the work performed by the department on day one. In 2017, our contracts were housed in multiple repositories and largely handled offline. The department's first priority was to implement a robust Contract Lifecycle Management (CLM) platform that could integrate with the company's CRM tool and automate the request for legal assistance as well as provide the department with a secure, searchable contract repository. No small challenge.

Throughout our digital transformation, legal department managers have needed insight into how their teams were using their time, for appropriate resource allocation and determining the time savings of our tech-driven tools. Through a combination of capacity tracking and the department's online operations, workflow, and communications platform – called BriefBox – managers are able to view matters their teams are working on in real-time – and their team members can view this data too. This enables the team to help each other out when certain colleagues are out of capacity and others have a bit of extra time.

BriefBox has gained new features and applications through DXC Legal's transformation. It forms the central platform used by every individual in the team, at every level and in every role worldwide. At the time of writing, the DXC legal team is made up of about 40 percent lawyers, one-third contracting professionals, and a mix of operational and technology support.

BriefBox also has a portal used by our internal customers to request and receive legal assistance and give feedback. The combined technology is a product that DXC Legal licensed and then tailored carefully to achieve its objectives. It now is the place where much of DXC legal's work happens and people work collaboratively, with features including:

- Contract lifecycle and obligations management;
- Matter management, business request and self-service, and workflow;
- Digital learning platform, contract risk assessment, online approvals, smart profiles, and SME finder;
- Talent management, including onboarding and capacity management;
- Dashboards, legal announcements, events, activity streams, search features, micro posts, and a chatbot;
- Internal and external collaboration spaces used by 100 percent of the global team;
- Outside counsel procurement and management; and
- Detailed reporting including on spend and performance.

In 2020, three years into our digital transformation journey, DXC's progress with digital implementation made a big leap forward. We saw a major impact on the delivery of value to the business – which was recognized by the business, our regional leaders, and our CEO.

What has worked in measuring value and demonstrating how we deliver it?

Below are four examples of how DXC Legal's digital transformation propelled the legal department forward, all related to measured and demonstrated value.

Higher quality, more readily available data

DXC Legal uses technology tools to integrate legal and contract management data from multiple tools and systems (e.g., SalesForce, DXC's contract management system, deal status data, and workflow data) and uses it to prioritize actions to manage legal risk, deliver the greatest value to the business, and allocate resources effectively.

The data we could produce in 2020 changed our ability to react in real-time, with a weekly report that every DXC Legal team member sees (typically by geographic region). It helped DXC to better capture opportunities, manage the company's obligations to customers, identify and address delivery weaknesses, and streamline how our legal professionals reduce business risk worldwide.

As the COVID-19 pandemic unfolded in early 2020, DXC sales, delivery, and finance has relied on legal for essential, high-quality information on new and existing contracts, as corporate clients across the world took action to manage COVID-19's impact. Our team was agile enough to provide force majeure and other essential information on customer contracts within 48 hours. That agility was based on teamwork to share data and what we were learning across each region, following time zones as the crisis unfolded.

Among our data advances in 2020 and 2021 are:

- Streamlined data collection on transactions and accounts;
- Deal wins/losses data automatically sent to bid teams and legal managers;
- Pre-litigation disputes tracked with data, including financial, cause assessments;
- Contract health indicators tracked in real-time, aged receivables, credits, claims;
- Improved focus on data aging with a weekly hygiene report; and
- Targeted data audits on randomly selected deals, disputes, and accounts.

Gains through digital contract risk assessment tool and online approvals

The Digital CRA contract risk assessment tool was launched in 2020. All legal professionals involved in contracts track and manage overall contract risk on Digital CRA by pre-defined risk category (e.g., liability, scope, term, termination). Users get specific guidance, examples, and favorites to use in the tool while updating contract risk and spending far less time on data input.

The Digital CRA tool (housed on BriefBox) replaces time-consuming manual assessments that were previously done in Excel. It gives DXC Legal a single standard that supports approvals of contracts worldwide – which in turn increases our efficiency, continuity, and performance in risk management.

Some of the benefits we have seen include:

- We can quickly provide new legal data that is mission-critical for business deal reviews.
- Real-time and auditable contract risk management – with reports to different levels of management in legal and DXC business units.
- We have greater knowledge and records of mitigations to reduce risk and disputes.
- Provides valuable data to DXC delivery professionals to act on issues and strengthen customer relationships.
- Leads to more profitable contracts.

Online contract approvals

In 2020 we piloted this new function – a natural next step after digitizing contract risk assessments. Using a new logic engine developed by our team, online approvals' greatest benefit is one location to request, respond, and track legal approvals on all contract risks. The results are:

- An auditable history of approvals granted/rejected/delegated;
- Notifications of approvals required and approval status, for better contract management; and
- Data gathered through global use of online approvals reduces data silos and improves the company's transparency and consistency in contract risk management.

Capacity management advances

In 2021, members of the DXC legal team gained the ability to better manage capacity through advancements to the BriefBox technology platform. The new tool enables team members to:

- Easily and efficiently update their capacity and view the capacity of our team members;
- Notify their manager of their current capacity; and
- Provide their profile and view those of their colleagues, with the ability to seek subject matter experts.

This feature helps individuals communicate their current workload quickly and efficiently, including automatic notification of certain events to the individual's manager. All legal team members update capacity weekly (or when there is a material change in capacity) on a scale of one to five, with emoji for each level.

Managers can view and take actions based on their team's capacity through this tool. They gain a more granular view of each team member's capacity, including over a period of time.

Since DXC Legal's operating model revolves around delivering legal advice, data gathering, and reporting, DXC Legal continually works to provide optimal productivity of our people. We aim to give individuals time to do work that is of higher value and more rewarding to them.

A culture that aligns people, technology, processes, and data

It was decided from the start that data must be at the center of the change process, right alongside DXC legal professionals' ability to adopt new tools and adapt their way of working to one where change is constant. We took a multi-faceted approach rather than a single solution, aligning technology, data, people, and processes.

An emphasis on data enables us to use quality data to inform decision-making at all levels of the department and, equally important, provide valuable data to the business. This is critical to ensure long-term value creation and performance of the legal function. The technology platforms we implemented use real-time data to manage the organization and we used the digital CRA tool to anticipate risk.

Since at various times data input time has increased for our professionals, we continually work to integrate data better to reduce data input burden. We also regularly share data with the team to show the knowledge made available through their efforts.

We aimed to use the data proactively to prevent issues from escalating to litigation and we coupled this with data-driven and integrated core solutions that would allow us to make faster and better-informed decisions.

Do not be led to think that this was a straight line of progress. Some of our tools didn't deliver as they should despite significant efforts, and we had to go back to the drawing board. Some proved very complex for our people to adopt – often because our training was unclear or inadequate, and some were overly labor-intensive for our team.

These are natural growing pains. We sought input throughout and made corrections to learn from inevitable mistakes. We worked with AI and automation and initially were surprised that AI generally was not quite delivering what we expected. Over time, we have had some success with both.

Transformation requires making mistakes. If you make no mistakes, it's a clear sign that your change is not bold enough.

How do we prove the positive impact of our digital transformation? Our internal customer satisfaction with our people proves it. Our data proves it. Our business colleagues recognize that excellent data on customer deals comes from legal.

Our ability to reduce costs annually as we improve productivity and performance proves the remarkable impact of digital transformation. DXC Legal not only met its cost reduction target from 2017-18, the first year following the merger, but we have also met budget forecasts and achieved year-on-year operating cost reductions every year since.

DXC Technology CEO, Mike Salvino, told *Financial Times*:

> *"I have seen its [DXC Legal's] business impact – for our people and customers."*[4]

Since DXC Legal's vision and operating model are geared around delivering legal advice, data gathering, and reporting, DXC Legal can now:

- Ensure optimal productivity of our people, giving them time to do more rewarding, higher-value work and also enabling managers to effectively manage resources for the first time using insightful and real-time data; and
- Report relevant data to the business that offers management insights into our customer contracts portfolio.

For the first time, we can now run risk analyses on a portfolio basis for the business. Our digital culture demands creativity, collaboration, ongoing feedback and change, inclusion and respect, and continual learning and development. Our pulse surveys show that our DXC legal team is highly engaged.

We still have great demand for better tools and advances in both data analysis and integration. Digital transformation has no final destination, it is a continuous process. We are already gathering information on recent developments in AI and other technologies that are creating new opportunities for us to bring even more – possibly exponential – value to the business.

Key elements of digital transformation for the general counsel to remember

It is a challenge for legal functions to deliver and demonstrate value to the business. First, because legal is often regarded as a "blocker", a function that says "no" too often. Secondly, because legal is perceived as a cost center rather than a value creator. It is often a low priority for investing, which creates budget pressures that can be an obstacle to implementing digital transformation.

Every general counsel should have a structured approach and measure progress and results, often on multiple projects progressing simultaneously. The progress must be repeatedly communicated across the team and the organization. Continuity and consistency are important, as well as data that the business understands and that matches expectations.

There will be a stage where all of the new technology that has been implemented must be integrated, and often integrated with other sources of data in the company. The general counsel should keep this in mind from the start – it will be helpful later on.

Tangible gains for the business come first. The transforming legal department should focus first on achieving major gains for the business, followed by advances in the legal department's capabilities. In DXC Legal's case, we also wanted to achieve measurable productivity increases and reduce external spending, and do that with a continually learning, fully-engaged team of legal professionals.

We recommend that every general counsel focus on these transformation fundamentals:

1. Use business-grade technology, continually integrated and updated to achieve more productive modes of service delivery and the ability to manage risks in real-time. This will greatly improve risk forecasting

and resource allocation. All with the overarching goal to better serve internal clients and the company's stakeholders.

2. Maintain a culture where the team members own and embrace the transformation and are motivated by continual change, learning, and improvement. Acknowledge that your approach will not work for people who are not interested in constant change and continually expanding or altering their approach to work. That's OK. It's a culture that demands resilience, effective teamwork, respect and care for others, and full transparency.
3. Understand that at every stage there will be actions needed to improve or integrate existing tech-driven tools and integrate other tools with tailored processes. The road will not be smooth, so it's important to celebrate successes along the way, and acknowledge when something must change. As you advance, it will be important to continually increase your focus on aggregating data from legal and business sources to conduct advanced analytics and AI to deliver continually improving value.
4. These principles deliver two key benefits – real-time data-driven insights and actionable content highly valued by the business. If DXC Legal's experience is any indication, these benefits contribute to customer satisfaction and retention. They guide our managers and their teams to do higher-value work and handle more sustainable workloads.
5. Think big. Most legal departments are under pressure to achieve continuous cost improvements. Securing funding to undergo the necessary holistic transformation can therefore be challenging. Despite this, the temptation to limit your project to incremental change must be resisted if true transformation is to be achieved.
6. Involve your people every step of the way. The mindset of your people is the difference between "surviving" and "thriving" in the digital transformation process – as author John Kotter put it in his book, *XLR8*.[5] Digital transformation requires a unique mindset and culture, and the people and talent to support that culture. Digital advancement demands acquiring additional cultural characteristics – regardless of whether one is a lawyer, a business executive, or an operations manager.
7. Leaders of legal transformation must seek out or develop people with a matrix of talents that include being agile, collaborative, inquisitive, creative, productive, innovative, customer-focused, upskilled, multidisciplinary, resourceful, resilient, respectful, trustworthy, passionate, data-driven, lifelong learners, and digitally aware. It can't be done all

at once, but it must be done incrementally and reinforced continually. Developing these sorts of skills among accomplished, well-trained legal professionals with diverse disciplines requires a desire to learn, intellectual curiosity, and persistence. It's not all about lawyers.

8. The most successful digital transformation projects involve multi-disciplinary teams who leverage the power of cognitive diversity to maximize the value the whole department delivers. DXC Legal's 2022 team is proud to have diverse disciplines all working together. Inclusive teamwork is a priority.

When DXC Technology's legal function was launched at the time the company was formed in 2017, we developed a talent roadmap. Elements of the roadmap that may be useful to general counsel are:

- Articulate and communicate the vision, with a strong legal department vision statement and consistent messages.
- Define and continually enrich the culture – align the legal function to the vision statement (constantly "market the culture" by rewarding high performance, listening to team members, taking the pulse frequently, and taking action in response).
- Remix as necessary – retain only legal professionals with a good work ethic, integrity, teamwork skills, required credentials, and an appetite for digital.
- Prioritize learning – make learning the "flagship product" with a focus on understanding skills that are essential to achieve the transformation vision.
- XLR8 – create leaders at every level, breaking down the hierarchy and conventional change management by developing people at all levels that take part in igniting and implementing change.

Practical examples of how we have managed and sustained the success at DXC Technology include:

- Actively celebrating successes;
- Permitting teams to experiment and support the implementation of their project concepts; and
- Fostering a collaborative environment of mutual respect.

We involve a revolving cohort of top performers to develop change agents throughout our organization.

Conclusion

Law cannot stay the way that it has been forever. Lawyers and leaders cannot expect to use traditional ways of working and to create sustainable, meaningful value for the business.

DXC Technology's legal department has invested, learned, and evolved to be a successful example of an integrated in-house digital legal function. The impact of digital in DXC Legal is evident in everything we do – technology, provider relationships, culture, competencies, efficiency, delivery, and data. This impact extends across legal, compliance, contracting, and strategic risk management. Our department members are very proud of how far we have come, and what we have learned and achieved.

The legal sector has few comprehensive examples of truly digital global legal departments. However, change is accelerating and there is encouraging evidence that a growing number of legal leaders are embracing digital transformation.

References

1 "Why Every Company is a Technology Company", Stephenie Stone, Forbes, 23 January 2017, www.forbes.com/sites/forbestechcouncil/2017/01/23/why-every-company-is-a-technology-company/?sh=5588220257ae.

2 "IT's changing mandate in an age of disruption", The Economist Intelligence Unit, 2021.

3 See e.g., "Prepare your legal department to support digital initiatives", Gartner Insight, 1.3.2019; and "The drumbeat of digital: How winning teams play", McKinsey Quarterly, June 2019.

4 www.ft.com/content/8c9b9629-4aaa-48e1-86d7-4ce1e01d56b6, 2 October 2020.

5 *XLR8: Building Strategic Agility for a Faster-Moving World, John Kotter*, Harvard Business Review Press, 2014.

Chapter 4: Legal operations as a competitive advantage

By Hans Albers, director, legal management consulting, Deloitte Legal, and Áine Lyons, SVP and deputy general counsel, VMware

Taming the final frontier of legal department modernization – legal operations hold the key

Many organizations are making strides toward modernizing the legal department for improved efficiency, cost effectiveness, and alignment with business strategy. Legal departments are recognized as one of the last areas of the enterprise to undergo operational and digital transformation. The importance of catching up with other areas of the business, such as finance, HR, supply chain, and IT, is no longer optional – it's an imperative.

The discrete modernization initiatives that have been launched often involve the implementation of technology point solutions for areas such as contract management, matter management, and e-billing. This tactical approach to technology implementation is one of the main barriers of true modernization – the lack of a technology strategy and roadmap is impacting many legal departments from delivering on the mandate from their enterprises to embrace digital transformation.

Moreover, while many organizations use advanced technology solutions within specific areas of the legal department, they may struggle to provide a holistic and integrative approach. As a result, their path to maturity modernizations stalls. When asked about key capabilities that indicate legal department maturity and sophistication (Figure 1), more than a few executives acknowledge that they "aren't there yet". Why not?

While all organizations' facts and circumstances are different, five distinct barriers to legal department modernization have emerged. Let's identify those barriers and show how they are often closely linked.

We'll also show that the data needed to break down these barriers and prove the case for effective modernization resides in legal operations – the people, processes, and technology that drive value and transformation in the legal department.

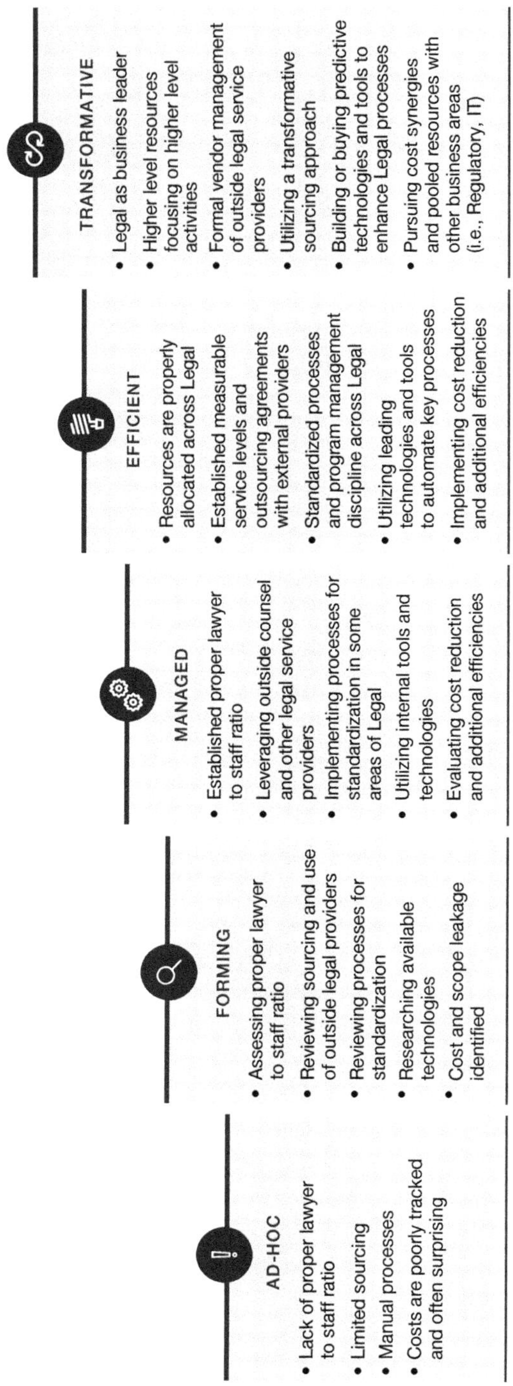

Figure 1: Legal Operations Maturation Milestones[1]

Barrier One: Consistent, sustained investments in modernization are hard to come by

An often-heard complaint is that legal doesn't have a budget for modernization and legal technology or that the general counsel (GC) expects other departments to drive the digital agenda.

General counsel often struggle to obtain funding as they lack the experience to build a business case for the needed investments. A legal operations function with financial expertise and budget planning responsibility can own this and work across the enterprise to influence leveraging existing enterprise tools and benchmark externally to justify the technology investment and build a business case for the impact and cost savings to the enterprise. Alternatively, this function can identify opportunities for cost savings elsewhere (typically in outside counsel spend) that can be re-invested in modernization.

Barrier Two: Functional silos are pervasive and disruptive

Litigation, discovery, corporate strategy, mergers and acquisitions, contracts, and ethics and compliance often operate independently, and their responsibilities can be both wide-ranging and complex. Leaders of these areas can be protective, and modernization efforts such as those involving technology advancement may be carried out in isolation from corporate IT or even other areas of the legal department.

Integration of legal technologies is often non-existent, preventing a clear line of sight across modernization efforts and impeding leadership's ability to leverage successes and innovations across the legal function to demonstrate enterprise impact. Legal department technology transformation needs to transform enterprise processes and move out of the silo.

Barrier Three: Data and metrics are often missing or inadequate

In many legal departments, leaders have only a general understanding of what their legal professionals are working on at any given time. However, workflows are typically not structured or governed across each function in a way that enables effective use of key performance indicators (KPIs) or metrics to evaluate, among other things:

- Individual and team performance; whether the most effective resources are being applied to high-risk, high-value activities; and
- How effectively legal budgets are being allocated internally or externally.

The great majority of legal departments do not view their data and metrics with a strategic lens. Most departments do not integrate their data with enterprise processes and don't use them to drive strategic discussions with their enterprise clients.

Barrier Four: Confusion reigns around knowledge management

Many organizations apparently mistake content or document management for knowledge management. The distinction between them has become much clearer as many legal professionals have worked from home during the COVID-19 pandemic. Gone were "water-cooler conversations" through which insights and knowledge have long been shared among legal professionals. The tendency to reinvent the wheel from one project to the next – a longstanding challenge in legal departments – has been exacerbated by the virtual work environment. Legal operations professionals can help resolve the confusion and embrace the requirement for knowledge management in the future workplace.

Barrier Five: Change management is often overlooked and undervalued

Reliance on established precedents for decision-making and weighing the resulting risks of those decisions are traits that are deeply embedded in the professional DNA of most lawyers. General counsel often aspire to manage change but typically don't have the skills or experience to do so. For many, there is little appetite for change, and legal modernization is a concept fraught with potential risks. Fixed mindsets prevail while growth mindsets are needed to drive transformation.

Change management is a discipline designed to address such concerns by clearly and consistently articulating the vision for and benefits of modernization and helping build buy-in and support through frequent communications. However, it is an often-misunderstood discipline and considered an unaffordable luxury. It is, however, fundamental to success of any attempt at transforming the operating model of the legal department.

Barriers often overlap and are interdependent

The five barriers described above can each be daunting and disruptive to tackle on their own. Combined, they will almost certainly prevent a legal department from making tangible, sustainable progress toward modernization goals. Ironically, clues about how to tear down these barriers and organize a cohesive modernization effort typically reside within the legal department.

If legal decision-making hinges on precedent and risk management, yet modernization assessments and roadmaps lack adequate and convincing details or proofs of concept, how can executive buy-in and support be expected? When siloed areas of legal departments don't go the extra mile to integrate their technologies and processes with data intelligence from those of other areas, how can they develop key performance metrics that might highlight potential operational improvement opportunities or, conversely, already-achieved modernization successes that might bolster their business case for additional funding and support?

Many lawyers and legal professionals would be willing to support new ways of working if they had the bandwidth or skill to make it happen. It can be a vicious circle, when even the tech-oriented lawyers who are eager to see change have such heavy workloads that there's no way for them to devote the time and learn the disciplines required.

Effective change management relies on facts and clear communications to convince people that a new way of working will be beneficial. Yet if siloed systems and processes persist, and a legal department has inadequate knowledge management, how can the facts and communications needed for change management be developed? Where can such clues be found? The answers lie within legal operations – the engine that drives value for the legal function and acts as a translator between the legal department and other parts of the enterprise. Legal operations leads the people, processes, and technology transformation strategy of the modern legal department:

- *People*. Those who do the work – i.e., who does what; where they sit in the organization; and whether the tasks they perform represent the highest and best use of their time, responsibility, and skills.
- *Processes*. How the work gets done – i.e., how tasks are executed step by step and how the product of those tasks flows from one person or group to the next.
- *Technology*. The tools that support the work – i.e., what current technologies are being used; what insights the data from those systems can provide about performance, cost management, and operational efficiency; and what additional technology tools might be adopted to enhance legal department productivity, cost-effectiveness, and alignment with business strategy.

The data that is available through legal operations can offer strategic insights on how to provide the right legal resources at the right time; demonstrate that work is being done by the right roles in the most cost-effective manner; increase productivity and speed; and help show that high-quality legal work aligns with business strategy and risk appetite. With such data, the legal department can begin to position itself as a better partner to the business and, in the process, prove the case for legal modernization.

Figure 2 shows how these three elements of people, process, and technology come together in the legal operating model "house" and how these are linked.

Starting with technology is not the answer

In the current environment, and given the amount of technology focused on the legal sector, it is not surprising that many GCs and their teams default to the belief that by adopting artificial intelligence, robotic process automation, or data analytics they will be able to cope with the speed of change and increased demands that are placed on the in-house legal function by other parts of the organization, their owners and regulators, and the public.

However, technology is only one component of the legal operating model, as illustrated on the next page. One of the common mistakes is the belief that new technology can fix a broken process. It is true that if you have a process, it can be automated. But it is important to take time to review and improve processes before automating them. Otherwise, you end up with an automated but still broken process.

Where to start?

> *"People cannot change their tidying habits without first changing their way of thinking."*
> Marie Kondo

We already mentioned the importance of change management and the critical element of getting this right from the start; you need to have a vision of the goal you want to achieve with your department. Increasingly legal can and is expected to be a strategic advisor and not just a trusted legal advisor. Adjust your way of thinking and challenge yourself and your team to be that strategic advisor. With this way of thinking, you need to define your strategy and make sure it aligns with the strategic imperatives of your business. Then articulate your why – what it is that you want to achieve.

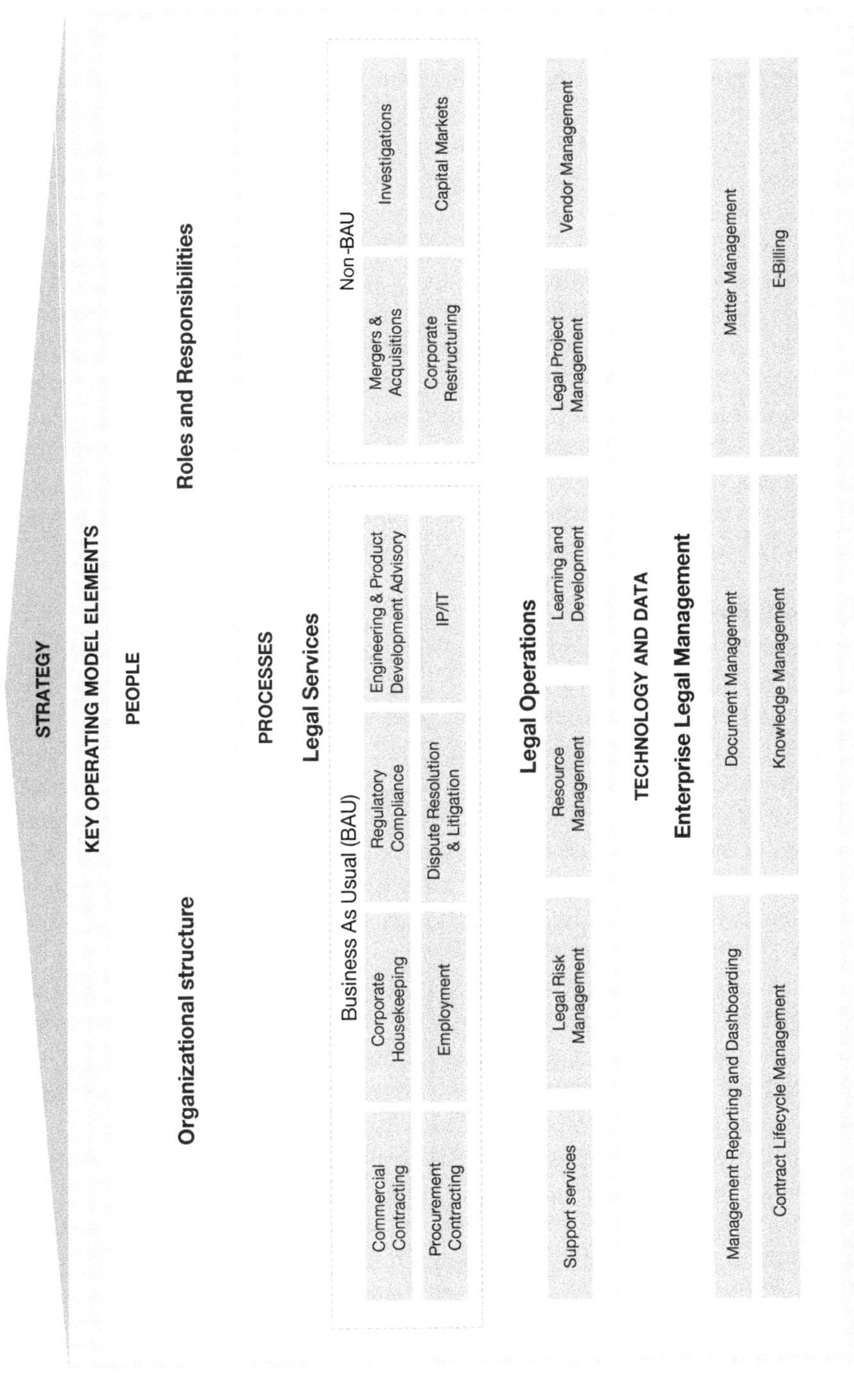

Figure 2: Legal Operating Model[2]

So maybe we can apply some "Marie Kondo" thinking to the world of the corporate legal department. By decluttering legal, we can add value and increase the competitive advantage. Think about what isn't adding value. What can you stop doing – what can and should you remove from your legal service catalogue? Then be diligent about getting rid of what you don't need or want.

We will describe how best to approach this and explain why legal operations needs to be in the strategic center of your legal function and how as a general counsel/chief legal officer (CLO) you can and must take advantage of the benefits of having a legal operations function within your organization.

A legal operations specialist or even an operations function can clean up, put things in order, and bring structure to your legal house. After years of looking after the business, things need to be sorted out so you can be more effective and efficient in the future. The time to do this is now, as things are sure to get more complicated and faster paced. This is even true for smaller teams or start-ups.

The value of data

Data is the foundation for everything legal modernization hopes to address, including process improvement, technology enablement, automation, service delivery, vendor management, and operating model refinement. By gathering, centralizing, and analyzing clean, accurate, and timely data about legal operations, decision-makers can build a clear picture about where modernization efforts will be most impactful. They can determine how and when to execute initiatives in an iterative or broad-based manner, with each project building on its predecessors. They can also develop insights on how to foster buy-in and, ultimately, adoption among key stakeholders, both within the legal department and across the business it serves.

The data collection and analysis process should focus on practical and tactical information about the activities being performed, the processes governing those activities, and the enabling tools. This information can be gathered in a variety of ways, such as through online surveys, outputs from selected administrative systems, and existing documentation.

Also important is the scope of data collected and analyzed. Limiting the focus to a specific functional group will only address part of the puzzle. An organization is usually better served by expanding the effort department-wide. Doing so can enable reuse of the data, fuel agile decision-making, and promote the development of actionable insights that can be leveraged on future modernization projects.

Moreover, by having the detailed picture that data collection and analysis provides, legal executives can make informed decisions about whether to take a "big bang" approach to modernization or an approach that focuses more modestly on low-hanging fruit and then builds toward more ambitious projects over time.

Traditionally, the legal department and the general counsel's role was to provide legal advice and solve unique and complex legal problems. Legal reviewed contracts, handled claims and litigation, made sure trademarks were registered, corporate entities were in place where needed, and regulatory developments were tracked. This was always done in close collaboration with external counsels that provided specialist advice without negotiating fees because they were longstanding trusted advisors that were always on call.

Today, data is the language of business. Legal and the general counsel will be expected to use KPIs and metrics to demonstrate if and how legal is adding value to the enterprise. Data can be used to support business cases and budget planning and for driving strategic business discussions on customer experience, deal velocity, and risk areas.

Strategy trumps all

Complexity in the business leads to an increased demand for legal services. However, throwing more lawyers and legal professionals at this complexity and increased workload is not a sustainable solution. A new way of thinking is required and an analytic look at the structure and processes of the legal department.

Although it is tempting – and more straightforward – to focus on one or more of the enablers, it is putting the cart before the horse. To evaluate where resources should be targeted, the GC first needs to define an operating strategy for the department that is closely aligned with the strategy of the enterprise. This allows the GC to put in place a governance framework to support the strategic objectives. The operating strategy will need to determine roles and responsibilities and define key results that contribute to enterprise growth. The operating strategy encompasses the role of the legal function in relation to the rest of the enterprise, and the responsibilities of the individuals within the department.

In our experience, few organizations have a properly articulated legal operating strategy that is communicated both within legal and in connection with the rest of the enterprise.

Lack of a clear strategy may happen because the department hasn't needed to articulate its strategy. Even where having an operating strategy is recognized as important, it is rarely urgent in the absence of a triggering event such as a merger (potentially turning two legal teams into one), a significant issue, a requirement to cut costs, or the arrival of a new GC. Other barriers to action include limited understanding of the possibilities that a new operating model presents, budgetary constraints, or a belief that what we have now works well enough – no need to fix what isn't broken.

To the extent a strategy exists, it has typically arisen by default in reactive response to the demands of the organization rather than being proactively thought out. It often resides in the heads of the legal function leadership rather than on paper. Without clarity on strategy, unsurprisingly the other components of the legal operating house (Figure 2) are not clear or succinct.

Defining the legal department operating strategy

The head of legal operations can and will often create the strategy, to make sure it is defined for the legal department. Obviously, not in isolation as this requires planning, discussion, and teamwork between the GC and their team but legal operations should own the overall process and the execution of the agreed outcome. To enable and empower the role to drive transformation, having this role report to the GC is optimal.

The choice of strategy to adopt depends on the overall strategy and risk appetite of the organization with which the transformed legal function's strategy and risk appetite need to be aligned. It will also be a tactical response to the expectations of many stakeholders beyond those employed within the department. These include the board to which the GC reports, other functions within the organization who rely on legal for the fulfilment of tasks and the delivery of services, and can potentially include the organization's own customers and strategic partners.

For example, if there is an underlying imperative to achieve efficiency gains or focus on risks and controls this will have a significant impact on the direction the strategy takes as it is developed. If the role or mandate of the GC is changing, this too may impact the strategy. Some organizations decide to have no legal team and outsource the fulfilment of their legal service needs entirely, which is one type of legal operating model, albeit entirely outsourced.

Roles and responsibilities

Clarity as to roles and responsibilities evolves from the chosen strategy and has often been lacking in more traditionally run legal functions. This has several undesirable consequences. These could include a lack of clarity as to where in the organization responsibility for relationships with the relevant regulatory bodies sits – is it in the legal, compliance, or regulatory affairs function, or is it in all three of these functions, depending on the topic?

Frequent lack of clarity around responsibilities within legal causes inefficiencies, because stakeholders may go to the wrong team member for assistance, which wastes the time of both parties. As the legal function transformation evolves, it is possible that a need for new responsibilities within the department is identified. This could be driven by additional specialisms in response to changes in the business model such as developing new products and services using the cloud or digital currencies. Depending on which of the enablers are areas of focus for the future, it is likely that new positions will be created within legal operations such as a legal technology lead, legal data scientist, legal process engineer, privacy operations, compliance operations, and environmental-social-governance (ESG) operations.

VMware: A legal operations case study

VMware is a leader in cloud computing, cloud infrastructure, and digital workspace technology. A global company, VMware is served by a 200+ member legal team across 36 countries. It's a diverse team comprising 40 percent legal professionals and 60 percent lawyers and is 50:50 men and women. Complementing an organization that accelerates digital transformation, VMware Legal developed multiple multi-year strategic plans closely aligned to VMware's business strategy and assumed a mantra of "*fearless legal innovators*".[3]

VMware Legal's mission is to "*drive innovation and power customer success through risk-smart, compliant solutions*".[4] Making that mantra manifest, VMware Legal has been recognized, inter alia, as 2015 ACC Value Champions, *The Financial Times* 2016 Most Innovative Law Department, and as the recipient of the 2017 George B. Vashon Innovator Award from the Minority Corporate Counsel Association.

As part of an innovation-focused company and as an industry-leading law department, VMware Legal wins awards for its innovative approach to work. It makes sense. The fact that it seems so natural obscures the deliberate design decisions and hard work that transformed the legal function from a collection of individual lawyers and legal professionals into a world-class operating unit.

In 2013, Áine Lyons transitioned from her position as EMEA general counsel to systematically build VMware's legal operations team. Below are some highlights of what that team, working in partnership with the

VMware general counsel and entire VMware legal team, have accomplished to date:

- Restructured VMware's legal value chain, including building internal capacity through strategic hires and developing a global legal services group dedicated to scaling transactional support. Transformed relationships with outside counsel through a comprehensive preferred provider program; and introduced legal process outsourcing to drive flexibility, scalability, and cost savings.
- Built a Diversity, Equity, and Inclusion (DEI) strategy with action plans for senior leaders to develop and grow a diverse team and an inclusive community where people can do their best work. Developed programs to support the team to stretch and grow careers as part of a modern legal function via targeted development plans, mentoring programs, and business, legal, and technical training programs.
- Reoriented the law department's focus on analytics and business intelligence to properly leverage legal expertise and support strategic decision-making from spend dashboards, KPIs, and budget forecasting to billing compliance, invoice audits, and staffing efficiency.
- Revitalized the law department's legal technology infrastructure for knowledge management, document management, e-discovery, e-signatures, dashboards, information governance, e-billing, and data privacy.
- Rebuilt the company's contract lifecycle ecosystem from initiation through retrieval to deliver a fast and simple contracting experience that inspires customer trust. Developed a One Customer Contract by streamlining and consolidating all customer-facing templates into one shorter, simpler template. Automated playbooks and a digital workflow cut cycle times and templates by 50 percent while reducing escalations by 74 percent. Contracts that used to require hours to identify (e.g., pending renewals) can now be identified in minutes.

The last bullet is a great example of the type of initiative where a sophisticated legal operations function can alter the service delivery landscape. Contract lifecycle management sits at the intersection of business necessity and classic legal practice. It is an excellent illustration of how the demands of volume, variety, and velocity can outpace available legal labor in ways that are directly detrimental to the corporate bottom line.

The four faces of the legal operations executive

Today's legal operations executive is multidimensional, bridging the world of operational efficiency and legal services delivery. Focused on strategy, process, budget, talent, and technology, the legal operations executive is increasingly operating at the highest and most impactful level of the legal function. In 2020, 68 percent of surveyed legal operations executives reported directly to the general counsel or chief legal officer – a percentage that is likely to have increased significantly since then.[5]

With the expansion of the role and responsibilities and the growth of the operations team, legal operations executives may be challenged to stay focused on the most strategic initiatives. As legal operations professionals continue to chart the path forward for this critical role, it may be helpful to consider the allocation of time between four critical "faces" – Strategist, Catalyst, Steward, and Operator.

The Strategist

The Strategist is responsible for defining the legal operations vision and clearly articulating the desired goals and outcomes. The strategist is a relationship-builder, a proactive thinker, and a strategic enabler and influencer, always working toward alignment with both legal department and business objectives.

Some responsibilities that may be associated with the Strategist role include:

- Align legal operations' priorities and resources with legal and corporate strategies to optimize costs and create additional value for the business;
- Anticipate and proactively develop a strategy to address operational, technological, and talent leading practices;
- Design the appropriate department operating and service delivery model;
- Articulate the value proposition of legal operations;
- Develop a capital investment strategy and budget that includes technology investment and a plan for external spend and fee negotiation; and
- Build strong relationships with internal and external stakeholders and other legal operations professionals and industry groups.

The Catalyst

The Catalyst drives for change with purpose and intentionality. For a legal operations executive, this role includes an emphasis on cultural change and the ability to lead others into new territory with a sense of enthusiasm and optimism. The Catalyst is a sensible disrupter, both self-aware and possessing a high degree of emotional intelligence.

Some responsibilities that may be associated with the Catalyst role include:

- Promote and cultivate a culture of innovation and lead change management efforts in the legal function;
- Drive continuous improvement through process simplification and standardization;
- Be a thought leader on innovation, technology, and leading practices for legal operations;
- Drive engagement by providing tech enablement that allows legal department leaders to work more efficiently and deliver more forward-looking outcomes to their business clients;
- Explore prototyping to develop and grow new ideas, either internally or through ecosystem partners; and
- Demonstrate commitment to work–life balance, diversity, equality, and inclusion as a role model for the legal operations team and the legal department.

The Steward

The Steward establishes trust through delivery excellence, working to protect the assets of the legal department, including both reputation and budget. A savvy Steward leverages business intelligence to enable a deep understanding of how the legal function delivers value and works to support and enhance that value creation through adept project management and an eye toward cost management. Some responsibilities that may be associated with the Steward role include:

- Oversee legal project management to execute tasks on time, within budget, and with quality;
- Develop a suite of standard program and project management approaches, playbooks, and tools for rapid delivery of projects through large-scale programs;

- Work with procurement to identify spending trends, potential cost savings, and efficiency opportunities;
- Partner with finance to understand the value of legal spend and develop accurate forecasting and reporting;
- Embed a data-driven mindset into the legal department; develop, monitor, and leverage KPIs to track success, demonstrate value, and enable the executive team's informed decision-making; and
- Develop and implement an ongoing vendor management program, including a preferred provider list of outside counsel and relationships with legal technology service providers and alternative legal service providers, as well as a plan to serve as a liaison between all the providers to drive the most value.

The Operator

The Operator is action-oriented, focused on enabling legal operations and legal department talent. The Operator is also skilled in understanding how to leverage technology to drive toward a more efficient and effective legal function.

Some responsibilities that may be associated with the Operator role include:

- Seek out the voice of the customer to assess the operational efficiency of the department;
- Evaluate the technologies that support the legal function; identify and implement technology solutions for the legal department;
- Identify whether technologies supporting legal are compatible and fully integrated with enterprise technologies, including enterprise resource planning (ERP), customer relationship management (CRM), and third-party risk management;
- Provide training for technology and process innovation;
- Establish common understanding of expectations, roles, and responsibilities among the legal operations team and identify gaps; and
- Refine the legal talent strategy; work with the legal HR partner to develop a talent strategy for legal that meets the future needs of the organization.

Although it may be helpful to think of the legal operations executive's priorities in neat categories, priorities often have components that span more than one face. For example, the priority "anticipate and proactively develop a strategy to address operational, technological, and talent leading practices" likely involves elements of the Strategist role, understanding (and potentially influencing) the legal department strategy. It also may touch on the Operator role, implementing and enabling technology and training for the legal team to help them move into alignment, as well as hiring and onboarding new talent.

In the same way, the priority of "embed a data-driven mindset into the legal department; develop, monitor, and leverage KPIs to track success, demonstrate value, and enable the executive team's informed decision-making" may appear to be a straightforward Steward priority. However, if the legal department has never used a KPI model and technology implementation is necessary to achieve the goal, this priority may also touch the Strategist and Operator faces, too. The four faces exist simultaneously, and the legal operations executive's ability to navigate each is interconnected.

The role of the legal operations executive continues to grow in importance, with an increasing range of responsibility within the legal function. To stay on track, it may be helpful to assess your allocation of time and regularly evaluate and select your top priorities. To be successful in the role, understand the four faces, and where you need to focus your time and energy, execute on your top priorities, and hone your critical resources.

No matter the size of the legal team, assessing and properly leveraging talent is a critical factor for success in the legal operations role. Legal operations functions that have the ability to hire and grow their departments may want to consider a wide variety of skills sets. Large legal ops departments typically have many different disciplines, including financial analysts, paralegals, business systems analysts, eDiscovery folks, and project managers.

For leaders of smaller legal operations functions, leveraging talent is still important, but more creativity may be required. The small legal ops team manager may, for example, leverage internal talent from the legal team, rotate top talent lawyers into the role, or look to other functions in the enterprise, such as IT, business operations, or other areas to create a role that has a dotted-line reporting structure into legal. An alternative is to hire people with a background in finance or business operations, but this requires them to learn about the specific demands of the legal department. That skillset contributes specific skills and attributes much needed for operationalizing legal services.

Conclusion

As the final frontier of operational and digital transformation for many organizations, legal modernization is happening; it's real and it's gaining momentum. However, it also faces serious barriers that are likely to place significant demands on legal executives, their departments, and the broader organizations they serve. Legal executives can benefit from an investment in assessing upfront the current state of its people, processes, and technology. The insights provided by such an exercise can help them design a modernization program that aligns with business strategy and delivers on expectations for service excellence, cost efficiency, and resource optimization.

The adoption of a legal operations function that has the full backing and support of the general counsel brings several benefits:

- Focus and time to develop and drive the strategy and overall planning and budgeting process of the department, adding discipline and various elements of expertise. Building business justifications for strategic areas of investment for the legal functions to drive greater business impact to accelerate growth priorities.
- Legal operations can take responsibility for running the legal department as a business, just as the other departments managing KPIs and key metrics and integrating them with enterprise data system to deliver holistic metrics that have a real business impact.
- Legal operations can bring together different expertise such as IT and legal tech, spend management, strategic planning, resource management, and knowledge management.[6] They can work across the enterprise to integrate legal more tightly with the business. A strong and strategic legal operations department doesn't consist of just lawyers but also other professionals with relevant expertise in areas such as finance, IT, data management, privacy operations, ESG, DEI, and communications.

As a general counsel in the 21st century, the reader will be expected to demonstrate that legal adds value to the business' growth and creates a competitive advantage. This cannot be achieved the traditional way by simply hiring more or better-qualified lawyers. You need to operationalize the departments and align the legal strategy with your company's objectives and demonstrate your impact leveraging metrics and data to do so.

And, finally, always keep the human element in mind. Inspire, engage, and develop your people. To bring your team on a transformation journey, you will have to gain their trust and open their minds to a new, more rewarding future where they feel valued and can do their best work.

References

1 Deloitte Legal Management Consulting report 2021.

2 *Ibid.*

3 VMware Legal Department.

4 *Ibid.*

5 Corporate Legal Operations Consortium (CLOC), 2020 CLOC State of the Industry Report, August 2020, p.12.

6 See for an overview of all elements of legal operations the CLOC Core 12: https://cloc.org/what-is-legal-operations/.

Chapter 5:
Leadership behaviors that distinguish great general counsel

By Kenneth J. Fredeen, general counsel emeritus, Deloitte (Canada)

Introduction

General counsel or chief legal officers – the titles will be used interchangeably – play critically important roles within their organizations. They navigate the world of business and law, always remembering that they are legal counsel to the corporation as a whole, with fiduciary and independence responsibilities that other members of the leadership team do not share. For instance, general counsel are members of the leadership team and yet are seen by the board as independent from management, working closely with the board to create and maintain an effective and efficient governance model.

Not all lawyers are cut out to be general counsel and some general counsel struggle or fail. This chapter explores in depth the small behaviors that make the difference and distinguish great general counsel from the rest.

Two authors who have reflected deeply on the role of general counsel are Ben W. Heineman Jr and E. Norman Veasey. Their books and articles are all worth the read, but I particularly recommend two books, *The Inside Counsel Revolution*[1] and *Indispensable Counsel*.[2] Ben Heineman refers to four character traits that complement the technical legal skills of a general counsel. To summarize:

- *Independence.* Expressing what is in the best interest of the corporation, at all times inculcating the values of honesty, fairness, candor, trustworthiness, and reliability within the corporation.
- *Courage.* Speaking out even as a lone voice.
- *Tact.* The ability to disagree without being disagreeable, knowing when and how to express independent perspectives.
- *Credibility and trust.* Critical for a general counsel to be successful in the role. Many of the behaviors discussed below are important for building that credibility and trust.

While these are important foundational traits for a general counsel, this chapter is more nuanced, delving into behaviors that distinguish great general counsel and lead to sustained long-term successful careers and teams. These behaviors are at times very specific, important to certain stakeholders though possibly not so much for others. They speak to character. This is not an exhaustive list and certainly readers will agree or disagree on them, but it is hoped that the list will cause the reader to think about her or his own behaviors and the impact these behaviors have on others.

Self-reflection

Self-reflection is a key behavior and starts with honesty, seeking out meaningful constructive feedback and even professional coaching. Hopefully this chapter will be a place for general counsel and aspiring general counsel to start with the simple question: "Do I do that?"

Of particular interest are how these behaviors impact the teams that general counsel lead. Team leaders know that to be successful, they need a great team alongside them, a team that is high performing and engaged. Strong talent will choose where they will work. Chief legal officers who are known to exhibit bad behaviors will have difficulty attracting and retaining strong talent and instead end up with team members with similar behaviors to their leader.

Sometimes, general counsel are selected from within an organization as part of good succession planning and have had years to learn, be mentored, and develop strong relationships within the organization and amongst the legal team members. At times, a newly appointed chief legal officer is an external appointment with no or limited corporate counsel experience.

The newly appointed CLO might have spent years honing their skills leading teams, studying, and learning from others, or they might have no experience prior to the appointment. Some general counsel have reflected that they learned what not to do from general counsel with poor people leadership skills. Others learned from and were mentored and coached by great general counsel. In all cases, the learning curve to become an effective general counsel is long and steep.

Being a great general counsel is hard but rewarding work, a 24/7/365 responsibility. The general counsel serves and interfaces with many different stakeholders – the board, the Executive, their teams, regulators, peers, customers, employees, competitors, and others.

General counsel have often been appointed to their roles because of their strong technical legal skills, not because of their leadership skills and in particular their people leadership skills. They don't necessarily have the behaviors that will lead to success in their new roles. Often, general counsel don't have the benefit of receiving constructive feedback on their behaviors – the good, the bad, and those that will lead to their demise. Hopefully this chapter will lead to reflection, honesty, and a desire to change, which will lead to better and more effective general counsel.

Successfully building and nurturing relationships

General counsel must develop strong trusting relationships with the teams they lead, the leadership team, the board, regulators, and other stakeholders. Each relationship is different but behavioral consistency is key. Certain behaviors will damage relationships, but sometimes leaders will act differently depending on who they are dealing with.

Maybe the most obvious behavior is what has been called "kissing up, but kicking down", where a general counsel is effective in managing relationships at senior levels but is a tyrant towards law department staff and other more junior employees. This behavior is easily identified by team members and leads to morale challenges and bad behaviors by team members.

Trust and integrity are foundational for a strong relationship, whether it be with team members, other leaders, or external stakeholders such as regulators. Integrity is simply doing the right thing when no one is watching. Trust can be broken in an instant or over time and, when significant, it is broken forever. The breach of trust can result from what is said or done in one or many acts, or from people observing the bad behaviors of the general counsel in response to one serious incident, or over time.

As the leader of the legal team, effective general counsel know that their own and their organization's success depends on a strong team of legal professionals who are supported, appreciated, and engaged. After all, the law department is at the hub of the business engine, connected to all facets of the enterprise.

The legal team can literally make or break the organization, if not cause reputational or business and legal risk. General counsel must earn and keep the trust of their teams, and the behaviors of the leader will determine whether or not this will be the case. When the legal team has an underground internal support system where employees speak their minds and share information about how they are being treated, compensated, promoted etc., the general counsel may have lost the trust and followership of the team and his or her tenure might be short-lived.

Perfection is impossible but the journey is worth it

Great leaders are constantly striving for perfection, knowing that it is impossible to be perfect but that they can always be better. Leaders are so easily fooled or lulled into complacency from the importance we place on titles, especially like the lofty general counsel or chief legal officer. Others will continually remind them of that, but great leaders know better and are not fooled into believing that they are as good as they need to be. Leadership is fluid and requires adaptation and constant reflection and learning. Certainly the title is nothing more than just that.

It is very easy for general counsel to become isolated, to surround themselves with chiefs of staff, a few direct reports, the Executive and others, leaving them to believe that everything is fine. This feeling of complacency can be seducing. It's very tempting for the "yes" chorus to be the only voices heard, quieting the voices of naysayers and truth tellers.

The general counsel who becomes disassociated from the team and loses touch with the "front lines" becomes vulnerable. She is exposed to having to answer the age-old question of "Where were the lawyers?" so often asked by judges, regulators, and the public following major corporate mistakes or failures. Staying grounded and in touch with the law department team members is a behavior that will pay dividends over time. It is critically important for reducing organizational risk.

This leads to a connected thought. General counsel take different journeys to the leadership role. Some of these paths are paved with silver spoons and privilege. Others have not enjoyed or experienced the same journey. An attribute of a great general counsel is that they both understand the privilege they enjoyed and certainly now enjoy, and have made the time and effort to learn about the journeys taken by others. This is a requirement for an inclusive team where every member feels their voice is welcomed and heard.

This caring, supportive behavior and continual learning is the characteristic of an inclusive, confident, empathetic general counsel who understands the benefits of an inclusive law department. We can't change the journey we have taken, but we can take the time to understand and learn from the experiences of others. That connection grounds the general counsel and creates a culture of safety and sharing.

Key behaviors

So, with all of this in mind, here are some of those behaviors we need to pay attention to.

"Do as I do, not as I say"

This is a guiding parenting principle that applies to general counsel. Though a general counsel should be good to her or his word, leaders do not always exhibit behaviors and actions that match their words. For instance, if a CLO espouses diversity and inclusion, or work–life balance, the actions need to follow – they need to walk the talk. Leaders need to set a positive example for others to follow. Examples are transparently and openly being absent from the office for family events, vacations, personal care etc. This gives license to team members to do the same.

The COVID-19 pandemic has given general counsel a virtual window into the lives of team members and others, in ways never imagined in the pre-pandemic world. There is an assumed trust that this personal information will not be used to someone's disadvantage (for instance, "he needs the job so I guess I can pay him less"). Prior to the pandemic, it was easy to hide or even mislead, but the pandemic has opened our lives to others.

Hopefully, general counsel have strengthened their empathy, transparency, and people support skills needed to lead teams in a post-pandemic world. General counsel must be more sensitive to the needs of what is important and necessary for members of their teams to thrive and remain engaged. This will be even more important if an organization has chosen a post-pandemic remote or hybrid working model.

The question is, will general counsel be able to adjust their leadership style and have the skills required to lead in a post-pandemic world? The new world of work will create great opportunities for those general counsel to build great law departments and build trusting relationships throughout the organization and beyond.

Share information

General counsel have access to knowledge and information with which they are trusted. Knowledge is power and sharing it with team members can be important for them to properly discharge their responsibilities. This is about trusting and valuing the work being done by team members. A behavior of selective disclosure or giving non-transparent instructions leads to mistrusting and non-engaged teams. Even better, including members of the law department in meetings with the leadership team or the board gives team members direct access to the information and positive exposure to leadership.

Professionalism

Team members pay close attention to, and often share, what and how general counsel speak of and treat others. Naturally, people will wonder if what the general counsel is saying about someone else is also being said about them. The failure of a general counsel to follow respectful professional decorum leads to a culture of fear, mistrust, favoritism and worse.

How the general counsel operates and behaves will become known and possibly very public at times of regulatory inquiries or other incidents. It's wise to approach the role as if actions will come under close scrutiny at some point. Professionalism also transcends the workplace. General counsel who let their guard down outside of work may pay the price with lost respect and broken trust and long-term damage to their careers.

A recent example of this was an inappropriate posting by a general counsel on a dating site, which came to the attention of his team. Respect is earned, not granted, and it would be difficult to be a team member of a leader with a behavior that challenges an expected ethical and moral compass. After all, general counsel are the ethical gatekeepers for organizations and the bar is high.

A prime example of professionalism can be found in how general counsel communicate in emails and texts. It is not just what is said, but how it is said. Sometimes this written correspondence sees the light of day, with career limiting consequences. General counsel who do not exercise proper professional judgment may eventually be required to answer to others, within or external to the organization – such as litigants or regulators. Consistent professional behavior is an insurance that this is not likely to happen.

Leading in a crisis

There is nothing like a good crisis for an organization, its leaders, and board to understand the value of a talented general counsel. It is an opportunity that will make or break a general counsel with so many eyes falling on how they act under immense pressure and with so much on the line. A calm demeanor is critically important. So is clearly communicating the plan to manage the organization through the crisis, effectively and efficiently communicating during the crisis, and of course managing the crisis itself.

These are all critical attributes of a successful general counsel. The board and executive will observe whether the general counsel is on top of the facts, has a plan leading to the other side of the crisis, and is capable and confident without panic. This is the greatest leadership opportunity for a general counsel and may also present the greatest risk.

So much of this attribute is dependent on the consistent behaviors outlined in this chapter. For instance, knowing the facts requires a proper process to find them. Fact finding evolves over a crisis and at times the truth is not comfortable.

General counsel who have created a safe and inclusive environment will be told the truth. This will allow the general counsel to make strategic and difficult decisions. Those attributes will not only build management's trust but also from the board, regulators, and other stakeholders. They will be more confident that, under the corporate legal chief's guidance, the right thing will be done, even if it is difficult or contrary to what others might think or want.

General counsel who find themselves in a crisis will reap the benefit of strong inclusive teams and a network of peers who will be helpful for guidance. That will make the difference for the general counsel so that they can act decisively and with a successful outcome in a crisis.

Moments that matter

Moments that matter (and won't happen again) are opportunities for leaders to exhibit behaviors that are needed in that moment. It is at these moments that the true character of the general counsel is exposed. Everyone is watching or will hear about it. These moments test the strength of the leader.

During the course of a career, there are many significant moments that matter which will impact the legal team and other stakeholders. How the general counsel reacts to bad news (a litigation loss, a mistake), their inclination to blame someone or something, being confronted with a personal crisis like a family or team member's illness or death – and everything in between – are all moments that matter. Sometimes these are seemingly insignificant moments for a general counsel, but hugely significant for others. This is where the important behaviors of being self-aware and empathetic become critical for an effective general counsel.

General counsel, and all leaders for that matter, have the power to impact the careers and lives of others. How we enter a room, who we greet, how we act and acknowledge others and their work, are moments that matter and require constant and consistent behaviors on the part of a general counsel. There are many reasons for general counsel to be distracted and have excuses for not being present for the moments that matter, but an important and distinguishing trait of great general counsel is that they are there, in that moment, not distracted by people or things, and have the time that is required to really listen and care.

When to lead and when to follow

Organizations look to the general counsel to lead, but great general counsel realize that there are times when they should not lead. There was a time when a top-down leadership style was accepted and encouraged. Not so today. General counsel need to understand when they must lead from the front (a crisis or significant event) and when to fall to the back and let others lead. This requires excellent communication and coordination across multi-disciplinary teams. Following, rather than leading, gives general counsel many insights, and also gives others experience and deserved recognition. Great leaders have the confidence and are comfortable not leading and even following recommendations from team members, letting them lead in their own approach and style.

Taking the bullet

There are many examples of general counsel letting others take the blame. This is easy for a general counsel to do in executive or board meetings or with other stakeholders. Blaming others is the easy way out for a chief legal officer, but the implications are long lasting. Great general counsel will establish an "I've got your back" culture and a reporting structure that allows for accountability but does not require a scapegoat. They understand that mistakes will happen and risk taking will result in failures and learnings. Ben Heineman has rightfully called out many general counsel for hiding behind ignorance and failing to take the bullet when that was what was called for. Responsibility ultimately lies at the feet of the general counsel. That ownership and understanding makes a big difference in creating a law department culture that is safe and collaborative.

Recognition, giving credit, and creating opportunities

This caring behavior should not be too much to ask of a general counsel, but often it is. Success should be shared, and a confident general counsel will easily give credit to others. Often that opportunity arises in a leadership meeting or before the board and team members will possibly ever know whether they were given credit for their efforts and success. But the board and Executive will welcome the chief legal officer acknowledging others and this act of humility and honesty is a behavior that will be appreciated. For the person getting the credit, it could be a career moment.

Putting someone up on that pedestal is not only important to them but team members who observe, learn, and understand that their hard work and skill will be recognized in time.

As mentioned earlier in this chapter, keeping the career development interests of team members front of mind is important as it builds followership, trust, and engagement. Knowing that your boss is looking out for you, not just himself or herself, is important for morale and productivity. Looking for opportunities for team members even outside of the organization is even better. Passing on jobs that might be of interest and encouraging staff to explore career options all lead to a happier and motivated team. After all, if you train your people to leave so that they have the skills and talent to work anywhere, when they choose to stay as part of your team, that is the definition of engagement.

Engaged teams play a critical role in creating a positive law department brand. The general counsel cannot be everywhere and how her or his office is seen throughout an organization is dependent on team members not only positively representing themselves, but all members of the team. With consistent good behavior of the majority of the team, a bad apple exhibiting bad behaviors is less likely to spoil the entire department.

Roll up your sleeves on Inclusion, Diversity, Equity, and Accessibility (IDEA)

Not that long ago, general counsel started talking about diversity. That evolved to inclusion, which then moved to a commitment to equity. Adding accessibility, the "A" in IDEA, is even better. Creating a diverse and inclusive law department might very well be one of the most important skills for a great general counsel, and lead to a lasting legacy.

It has been wonderful to observe the leadership of general counsel on IDEA with their teams, within their organizations, and within the legal profession. There are many great examples of general counsel walking the talk and setting the example to be followed by others. These general counsel have taken the time to be curious and caring of others and the legal profession is so much better for it.

Observe great legal leaders and you will see them spending time with people not like themselves, staying to the end of a diversity function, mixing it up with folks, being human and approachable. They circle themselves with diverse people and are not only IDEA leaders but use their spending powers to create a more diverse and inclusive legal profession.

I want to end this part with a special call out to the letter "A". The inclusion of people with disabilities in law departments, law firms, and within the legal profession is maybe the "last frontier" of diversity and inclusion. People with disabilities represent 20 percent or more of our populations[3] and yet we have much to do to improve their inclusion in the legal profession, the economy, and our societies. The legal profession needs to do a better job of employing and including legal professionals with disabilities.

A great general counsel understands that hiring, retaining, and promoting legal professionals with disabilities is not only about equity and fairness, but about innovation, retaining top talent, team building, and success. The focus on DEI is great, but it needs to be IDEA for there to be true diversity and inclusion. Understanding and acting upon this is both a behavior and a skill great general counsel have.

Self-awareness and selflessness

These are two different things but are connected and are important behaviors for a successful general counsel. A self-aware general counsel will be more successful. Being able to look in the mirror, critically evaluate oneself, and seek out truthful and meaningful feedback so that behaviors can be adjusted is an important attribute for general counsel and their teams. It requires constant vigilance.

Likewise, being selfless is also important. General counsel did not get to where they were without a lot of hard work, maybe some luck, but also incredible drive. Once in the role, adjusting to being selfless will not necessarily come naturally and yet, it is an important attribute for a great general counsel. General counsel who think first of "What's in it for me?" will ultimately create an environment and culture where self-interests will always come first, for everyone. A general counsel will set the tone and culture, not only within the law department, but within the organization. Think of general counsel you respect, and it will be someone who freely gave of time and self, not of self-interest.

It is important to add here, that as the general counsel role grows and becomes more complex and demanding, that the general counsel must take time for personal care and give him/herself oxygen first, so that they are able to help and support others.

Maybe this is obvious, but it is worth highlighting. A law department mission and culture of serving the business and supporting each other reduces the risk of workplace toxicity with a culture of competition and internal fighting, where team members work to exhaustion and burnout. General counsel can nip these behaviors in the bud by modeling great behaviors.

Active listening and speaking last

Lawyers are trained to work through problems and find solutions, but general counsel understand that others will have perspectives and ideas that need to be heard before a final decision can be made. We know that once the leader speaks, the tone and the direction of the meeting changes. A general counsel who speaks more than he or she listens will miss out on important information needed to make the best decision.

It has been said that we have two ears and one mouth for a reason. Listening is a key attribute of a great general counsel, but a great general counsel also needs to encourage discussions and voices that might be kept quiet. Diverse views will lead to a better decision being made and encourage all opinions and facts to be put on the table. General counsel need to listen, challenge, be curious and ask questions, be open minded, encourage debate and when all has been said and discussed, agree on a course of action or a decision. It sounds easy but we don't live in a perfect world with the luxury of time. A distracted general counsel, speaking first or too much, excluding opinions for whatever reason, leads to poor decisions and demoralized teams. Great leaders know that diversity in all its forms in an inclusive work environment leads to better decision making. Bad behaviors will stifle this culture of inclusive discussion and debate if the general counsel is not vigilant.

Successors and predecessors and what they say and do about the other

Whether a general counsel recently served in the role or recently took on the role, how they act and what they say about the other is a measure of a general counsel's character. No doubt the successor will want to do things differently and, equally true, the predecessor will be proud of her or his accomplishments. But both are vulnerable and need the respect and support of the other. The mutual interest should be in each other's success and the success of the organization they served or are now serving. Self-interest is not in the interest of anyone.

Speaking skills: don't be boring

Great orators are not born. They spend countless hours practicing and never feel that they have done their best work. They self-analyze, seek out constructive feedback, and pay close attention to their audiences.

Unfortunately, there are too many times when general counsel speak too much, read from their notes, fail to communicate effectively, are distracted, don't connect with the audience, or are downright boring. No one has had the nerve to tell them. The art of effective communication often requires professional training and general counsel must make that a priority for themselves and their teams. After all, the content they are communicating is important.

There is an added risk for general counsel and their teams; legal bafflegab. Successful general counsel communicate complicated legal issues in a way that non-lawyers can understand, relate to, and act upon.

Humor, humility, and truly caring

Maybe these three concepts are not connected, but they are important behaviors for general counsel, and often they are found in the leaders we respect. General counsel have daily opportunities to set the mood for others, whether it be their team or amongst colleagues on the leadership team. General counsel do not have to be comedians, but they do need to be sensitive to the coolness or the warmth in the environments they find themselves. Sometimes general counsel are leading a meeting on a difficult topic, a significant risk, or piece of litigation. General counsel set the tone and the approach. We have all been in meetings where the leader arrives late or is distracted by other things, business or personal. Those meetings are different and less effective in terms of collaboration, sharing, teamwork, and problem solving. General counsel set the tone for how others will act, feel, and communicate.

Leaving meetings aside, general counsel have numerous daily opportunities to add humor, make people feel good, exhibit humility, and truly care about the people they are interacting with. If we think of great leaders, we think of this one thing that makes them stand out – they cared.

Protecting others' wellness and building personal resilience

The old saying "You can't help others if you are not caring for yourself" is so true. General counsel need to ground their own wellbeing and balance so they can not only help their teams and other leaders, but set a lived example of a successful, healthy career. Team members will observe the general counsel's actions carefully. General counsel need to be vulnerable and honest, knowing that they don't need to share what they had for breakfast, unless they almost died from eating it! General counsel know that team members struggle at times and that they might both need support and accommodation.

Service leadership and being accessible to your team and others

Great leaders serve. For general counsel, that is service to their client and to their teams, being there for them, and understanding that there are things that can be done for them that help them do their jobs better. Part of that is being accessible to them. Structures and reporting lines can impede access. Creating a culture of openness, sharing, giving, and serving each other is a culture the general counsel can create. Watching for and acting on behaviors that detract from this culture is the job of the leader. A law department culture of service is important for many reasons, in particular for the success of the organization.

Conclusion

It truly is the case with general counsel that it is the small things that matter. Strong legal technical skills are assumed but it is the small behaviors that demonstrate more distinctive strengths or weaknesses. These behaviors can often make or break a general counsel.

A general counsel who is not attuned to their own behaviors has the title but not the respect and followership so critically important for their success. The behaviors of successful general counsel today are different. Leadership skills are essential. There was a time when law departments were driven from the top down. Now we know better, and that is a good thing. General counsel who fail to recognize their good and bad behaviors will not achieve their full potential. No one is perfect, but at least we can strive for greatness.

References

1 *The Inside Counsel Revolution: Resolving the Partner-Guardian Tension* (2016), Benjamin W. Heineman Jr.

2 *Indispensable Counsel: The Chief Legal Officer in the New Reality* (2012), E. Norman Veasey.

3 https://www.rod-group.com/sites/default/files/2020%20Annual%20Report%20-%20The%20Global%20Economics%20of%20Disability.pdf

Chapter 6: Best supporting act – how adaptive legal functions are embracing technology

By Isabel Parker, executive director, The Digital Legal Exchange

A lot has changed over the past two years. Our personal and professional lives have been upended by the Coronavirus pandemic, causing organizations and individuals to re-evaluate their purpose and to work in very different ways. There is a shared recognition that the stability that we once regarded as our right is not something that we can take for granted. As the world begins to emerge from the worst ravages of the virus, and we look for a return to "normal", we should be wary of complacency. Recent research suggests that managing disruptive change is now the single most pressing challenge for both individuals and organizations. In the words of John Kotter, the godfather of organizational change:

> *"A focus on the pandemic as a once-in-a-lifetime phenomenon can lead us to be passive and miss the most important lesson: that this crisis is not an aberration but a spoke in a trend that has long and deep roots."*[1]

Becoming a digital, adaptive organization

To thrive and grow in this new, volatile world, organizations need to rethink their corporate toolkit. Kotter argues that the approaches that served so well in the past – traditional top-down strategy formulation and execution, growth through M&A, management through hierarchy, cost control through restructuring – are no longer sufficient. The organizations that emerge as successful will be wired differently, defined by an adaptive culture that enables them to respond quickly to change.

Technology has a critical role to play in building and supporting an adaptive organization. The right technology solutions, implemented in a strategic way to support an overarching vision, can help to make organizations more resilient and agile. However, investment in technology alone is not enough. To become more adaptive, organizations need first to reimagine their ways of working, their customer and employee interactions, and their culture for a digital age. In short, they need to commit to holistic digital transformation. Technology is central to digital transformation, but is only one part of a wider, multi-faceted commitment to what is a:

> *"...customer-centric, cross-functional, change journey that leverages technology, skills, data and metrics to evolve an organization's business and operating model in order to create (and capture) new forms of value."*[2]

At the enterprise level, most leading corporations now recognize that digital transformation is both a pressing strategic imperative and a potential source of significant value. Compare the results of a 2017 McKinsey survey on digital adoption with the results of the same survey repeated in 2020. In 2017, around half of respondents ranked cost savings as one of the most desired objectives of investment in technology. In 2020, however, *"only ten percent view technology in the same way; in fact, more than half say they are investing in technology for competitive advantage or refocusing their entire business around digital technologies"*.[3] For many leading organizations, digital transformation is not just a key part of the strategy – it is the strategy itself.

The legal/business disconnect

As digital transformation accelerates within the business, legal remains the last piece of the enterprise transformation jigsaw. This can be a source of frustration on both sides. The business wants the legal function to change, and the legal function recognizes the imperative for change – but there is a disconnect between the expectations of the business and the reality on the ground for legal departments. A survey commissioned in 2021 by EY Law and the Harvard Law School Center on the Legal Profession neatly illustrates this disconnect. According to the survey, 61 percent of CEOs are pushing their legal teams towards a more data-driven approach to risk management. However:

- One in every three law departments surveyed report not having the technology they need to do their job; and
- 97 percent of GCs report facing challenges in securing budget for investments in legal technology.[4]

Our research at the Digital Legal Exchange confirms this picture. The Exchange digital alignment survey, a mirrored survey completed by members of the legal team and their business colleagues, assesses the importance and performance of the legal function against 35 indicators. It is designed to reveal areas of alignment and disconnect between legal and the business. The aggregated results show a consistent disconnect between what the business wants and what legal functions prioritize, as shown in the figures below.

Legal functions could dramatically improve their use of digital tools

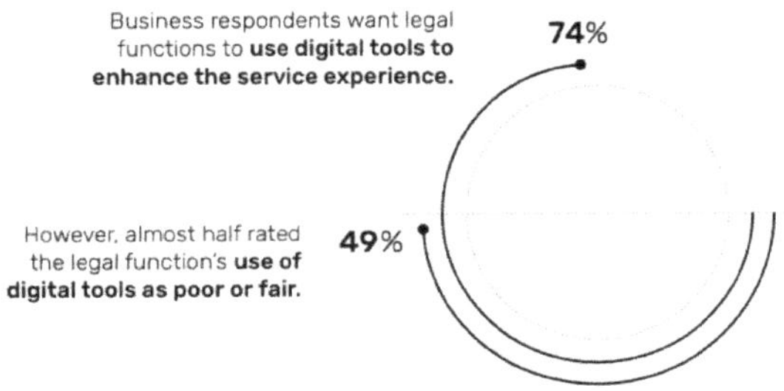

The legal function's metrics success should align with business goals

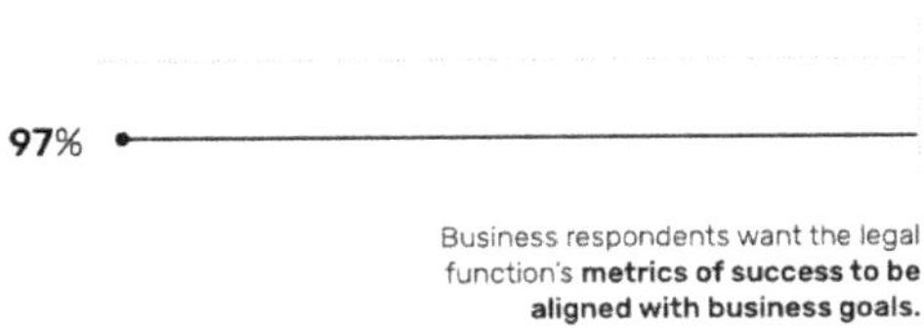

// *If legal functions are to help their businesses achieve their objectives, they must measure their success in the same way as the rest of the business.*

The business wants its legal function's metrics of success to be aligned with business goals. Almost all (**97%**) of business respondents said this was moderately to extremely important, and over half (**52%**) said it was extremely important, compared with only a quarter of legal function respondents.

Often, legal functions remain focused on measuring and reporting costs and savings rather than revenue or value generated. This makes it difficult to secure budget to fund transformational technology changes, and can be demotivating for legal function members in the longer-term.

These insights demonstrate that the business is pushing legal towards more digital delivery and demanding a legal function that is fully aligned with business objectives. The implications (both for legal departments and for the enterprise) of not addressing the legal/business disconnect are serious. A successful enterprise digital transformation cannot be achieved in a piece-meal way – it requires all functions in the organization to commit to the change. Our members at the Digital Legal Exchange tell us that for the legal function, demonstrating value to the business is one of the highest priorities.

However, demonstrating value is becoming increasingly challenging. The legal function's remit is expanding, but cost pressure remains intense. Something has to give; legal needs to commit to holistic digital transformation if it is to realize its ambitions and satisfy business demands.

Legal departments – "eager but not ready"

Why is the pace of digital change in corporate legal departments so slow? The prevailing view has always been that the legal department itself is the barrier to progress. Legal was traditionally viewed as the "department of no", a risk-averse business blocker. Legal did not have the right mindset; GCs, we were told, did not feel empowered to drive digital change and were not confident in their capabilities to sustain it.

Our research at the Digital Legal Exchange suggests that this is changing. At the end of 2021, the Digital Legal Exchange commissioned a private members survey, Benchmarking Digital Agility, designed to help members assess their digital maturity against that of their peers. The survey results demonstrated the degree to which legal functions' understanding of digital transformation has matured. For example, our survey found that:

- Legal functions recognize that close integration between legal and business is critical for digital transformation to be successful (two-thirds of respondents viewed business integration as a more important transformation objective than reducing legal costs).

Legal functions' understanding of digital transformation has matured

Our survey shows that legal functions are developing a sophisticated understanding of what digital legal transformation involves and the value a transformed legal function can deliver to the business.

Three key data points demonstrate this development:

1. Legal functions see **business integration as critical to success**.
2. Legal functions recognize that transformation is **within their capabilities**.
3. Legal functions understand that legal digital transformation is not just about technology: that it is a **holistic undertaking** requiring effort across all areas of the business.

The **three highest ranked concerns for current legal goals** (two thirds of respondents):

23%	23%	21%
Protect and realize core elements of enterprise value	Integrate more deeply with the business in real time	Demonstrate the value of legal to the business

The three **lowest ranked obstacles** to success:

1. We don't feel empowered
2. Legal is perceived as a blocker
3. High turnover from our teams

Allocation of legal functions' digital transformation efforts over the next 12 months is **evenly split across the four critical transformation components**:

Data and insights – **Automation and enablement** – **Culture and people** – **New ways of working**

- Legal functions recognize that transformation is within their capabilities (the traditional obstacles (such as legal being perceived as a blocker or legal not feeling empowered to change) have diminished in importance).
- Legal functions also recognize that legal digital transformation is a holistic undertaking across all areas of the business – not simply a technology program.

The responses to the survey suggest that legal functions are becoming more customer-centric, are looking to serve the business better, are growing in confidence in their capabilities to deliver digital change, and are realistic about the scale of the transformation ahead. These are very positive foundations for successful transformative change. However, there are two caveats to this positive picture.

- Firstly, Digital Legal Exchange members are senior legal and business leaders at large multinational corporations who are, in general, progressive in their mindset. We should factor in a little pro-digital bias; not all GCs (or all organizations) have the same growth mindset.
- Secondly, even though attitudes to digital transformation are maturing, legal functions are still challenged to move at speed. Bjarne Tellmann, Exchange member, faculty advisor and GC of GSK Consumer Healthcare (recently renamed Haleon in anticipation of its spin-off from GSK plc) recently co-published an article with fellow Exchange faculty advisor Michele DeStefano. Entitled "Don't Let the Digital Tail Wag the Transformation Dog: A Digital Transformation Roadmap for Corporate Counsel", the article is based on interviews with 25 GCs and chief digital officers of multi-national companies about how they are approaching digital transformation. The conclusion of the paper is that corporate legal departments are "eager but not ready":[5]

"Although GCs are attempting to digitally transform their legal functions, there remains a gap between the objective and the reality… despite their intentions and efforts, most in-house legal teams are failing to keep pace with the complexity and accelerating rate of DT."[6]

Our Exchange survey supports this conclusion. Our survey asked respondents to assess their digital maturity across four critical maturity

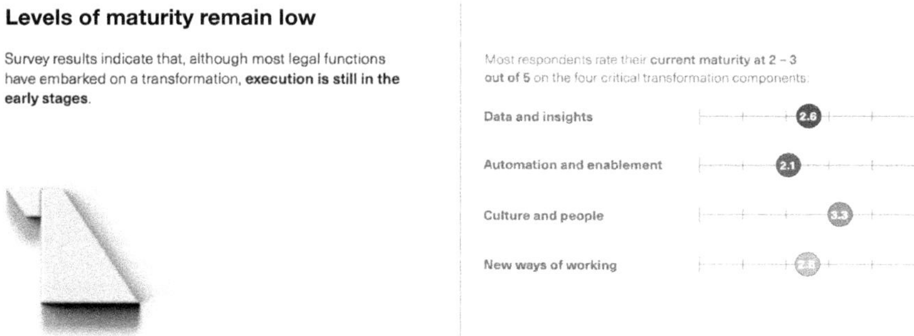

components: data and insights; automation and enablement; culture and people; and new ways of working. Levels of maturity across all four components were low.

This was particularly acute when it came to implementation of technology. Automation and enablement (which we defined in the survey as the use of technology to reduce or eliminate high volume, routine work) was the lowest scoring category. This was something of a surprise. Automation of routine legal work is often the starting point for legal digital transformation efforts, as the business case (increased efficiency and freeing up lawyers for more complex legal work) is comparatively easy to make. We would have expected legal functions to have made the most progress in this area. When it comes to use of more sophisticated technology, such as artificial intelligence, the picture is even more stark. Use of artificial intelligence had an average maturity score of 1.9 out of 5 – the lowest score across all categories in the survey, demonstrating that, despite the hype, AI is not being consistently used by legal functions as a standard part of workflow.

Other studies support the fact that use of technologies – sophisticated or cutting edge technologies in particular – by corporate legal teams is limited. In general, technology is being applied to make the legal function more efficient and effective, rather than to support the transformation of the legal service delivery model or to identify opportunities for revenue growth:

> *"As our GC interviewees explained, for them, going digital means 'technology stuff for efficiency' or 'sensibly using tech to make the department a more effective and efficient provider of legal services' to enable them to spend more time on the strategic work that matters."*[7]

Despite the push from the business for the legal function to digitally transform, and the growing confidence and maturity of the legal function, it still appears to be the case that strategic technology adoption amongst corporate legal teams is low.

The three barriers to progress

If legal departments are indeed "eager but not ready",[8] what is holding them back? Why have most corporate legal teams not followed the lead of the wider business and embraced technology as part of a holistic digital transformation? Our view at the Digital Legal Exchange, based on interactions with Exchange members and faculty advisors and our own research into the market, is that progress is being hampered by three (interrelated) challenges:

1. Data

There is insufficient data shared in the market to help leaders envision what a digitally transformed legal function could look like. This is unsurprising – there are still very few legal teams that have made measurable, tangible progress towards holistic digital transformation. Without examples of best practice or organizational archetypes to emulate, corporate legal teams can struggle to develop a "North Star" to guide their vision and strategy. To illustrate the point: how does a GC create a strategy for transformation of the litigation team when they do not have a clear vision of what digital litigation could look like – and what is achievable from a technology perspective? In the absence of a goal to aim for, legal functions often struggle to approach their digital transformations strategically. Instead, they make investments in technology point solutions without first thinking through the underlying cultural, structural, and organizational issues that need to be prioritized as part of the transformation. Tellmann and DeStefano's article presents (and critiques) a three-phased digital maturity framework to illustrate how legal departments in multinational corporations typically approach digital transformation – by introducing new technologies before the "non-digital foundations" of the department have been transformed together with business clients. This approach is problematic:

> *"GCs often find themselves forced to undertake profound organizational, structural, behavioral, and cultural changes after new technologies have been rolled out (sometimes unsuccessfully). This post-hoc approach (that leaves client-centricity and change management last) is disruptive, adds unnecessary cost, and threatens the credibility, viability, and timing of the entire DT effort."*[9]

To course correct and plan for a successful technology implementation, corporate legal teams need more examples of best practice from the legal functions that are leading the pack in digital legal transformation.

2. Value capture

Digital transformation is not a project or program with a beginning and an end. It is a multi-year investment that requires sustained financial and leadership commitment; it needs to become part of business as usual. Any multi-year investment requires a business case that clearly articulates the costs that will be incurred and the benefits that will accrue to the business. Because of the data challenge (described above) and because so few legal functions have successfully transformed, the benefits are not always easy for legal functions to identify. Precisely what is the "size of the prize" if a holistic digital transformation is thoughtfully planned and executed? The results of McKinsey's most recent Global Survey (undertaken during 2021) emphasize the importance of setting an overall financial target for transformation. According to McKinsey, this can only be achieved by undertaking a "comprehensive, fact-based assessment of the business to identify opportunities for improvement":[10]

> *"The more thoroughly that an organization uses facts to assess the maximum financial benefits it can achieve from a transformation in the first place, the more confidence leaders will have in setting and pursuing ambitious yet realistic targets that reflect the transformation's full potential."*[11]

The scale of this assessment can feel overwhelming to many corporate legal functions – particularly given the lack of reliable benchmarking data to help set realistic parameters and targets. Corporate legal teams need assistance (informed, again, by examples of best practice) to help them to formulate a business case that captures the value of a digital transformation.

3. People and talent

Digital transformation inevitably involves investment in technology. However, as noted above, it is now generally accepted that technology is not the right starting point. Instead, a successful digital transformation puts people and organizational change at its center. Digital delivery demands a new way of working, which in turn requires a new mindset. An ambitious goal for transformation is meaningless if it does not resonate with the people that need to execute on it. In addition, new ways of working require new skillsets, beyond technical legal excellence. This means multi-disciplinary teams of lawyers, legal operations professionals, developers, product managers, data analysts and data scientists, even organizational psychologists – skillsets outside the traditional competencies of the traditional in-house lawyer. With a global talent shortage for digital skills, corporate legal teams need to work hard to find the right talent. Skills do not always have to be sourced externally; our recent Exchange survey revealed that respondents have a high level of confidence in the digital capabilities of the legal department, with 81 percent of respondents reporting that they have digital talent as part of their existing teams.

Meeting the challenges

The barriers to progress are real, but they can be overcome. Momentum for change is building; our survey at the Digital Legal Exchange shows that a significant majority (88 percent) of members have already formalized and started to execute on a digital transformation roadmap.

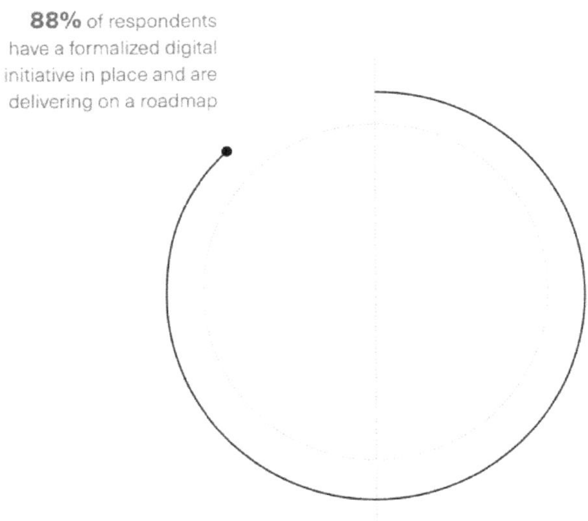

Gartner, in its 2021 Predictions for Corporate Legal and Compliance Technology, is bullish about how legal will transform over the next five years:

> *"...the next five years will see leading legal departments progress more quickly than most to an 'anything that can be automated, will be automated' stance. The accelerated pace for legal departments versus other functions reflects a more primitive, highly manual, starting point compared to other departments. Pent up demand, along with the rising potential of emerging technologies, such as artificial intelligence, machine learning, etc. to digitize the typically high occurrence of paper driven processes and collaboration in legal departments, will bring a relatively quick transformation for legal."*[12]

It is certainly true that the rewards for legal departments that approach technology investment in the right way, as part of a strategic and holistic digital transformation, could be really significant.

Examples of best practice

One of the three barriers to progress noted above is an absence of success stories to help legal departments envision what a digitally transformed legal function might look like. At the Digital Legal Exchange, our mission is to help corporate legal departments accelerate legal digital transformation in a way that is integrated with the wider business. To help achieve this mission, we have created a community of peers who share openly with each other the challenges and benefits of legal digital transformation. We share below some examples of best practice from our Exchange members. These corporate legal teams are leading the pack; they are adopting new ways of working and new service delivery models and embracing technology in support of these new models, all as part of a holistic digital transformation, creating value for the wider enterprise in the process.

Using cutting edge technology to transform collaboration

Long before Facebook rebranded as Meta, the legal department of one of our members (a multinational enterprise information technology company) was exploring the power of virtual reality (VR) to transform organizational collaboration. The pandemic catalyzed a new way of thinking and working within the legal department. The legal leadership recognized that video conferences were not sufficient to help those working remotely feel included, or to enable them to collaborate and innovate effectively. The legal team set up a task force to test the boundaries of VR for business purposes, allowing teams access to "persistent rooms" on a 24/7 basis, in which they could collaborate by reviewing documentation together, adding post-its with their ideas, and brainstorming solutions. This approach delivered significant business and inclusivity benefits – ensuring that every individual, regardless of where they are in the world, gets a "seat at the table". This is a powerful example of legal leading the charge, delivering value to the business and leveraging technology strategically to support new ways of working. In the Exchange member's own words, *"the legal department… is convinced that VR will transform the way that organizations collaborate and is now running several pilots with individuals, from all over the world, that are using VR to enhance their practices"*.

Adopting Agile ways of working

A number of corporate legal teams, particularly those in the financial services and TMT sectors, are looking to transform the way the legal function delivers to the business by adopting Agile ways of working. One of our members (a multinational telecommunications company) has committed to Agile within the legal department, to support a business that itself works in an Agile way. Adapting Agile principles for legal delivery is not a straightforward exercise. It involves breaking down organizational siloes, encouraging lawyers to work as part of multi-disciplinary teams (alongside the product or business teams that they support), and focusing on customer centricity – keeping both internal and external customers in mind when shaping the organizational and delivery model for the legal team. This Exchange member completely disrupted the traditional organizational structure of the legal team, reorganizing to work in the following ways:

- Tribes (teams with end-to-end accountability for significant areas of the business, such as privacy);
- Clusters (sub-sets of a Tribe, focused on a particular area of delivery – for example, product management);
- Chapters (teams organized around areas of leadership and development); and
- Squads (teams organized around individual topics, such as Cloud adoption).

The benefits of the Agile reorganization for the business are proving significant, providing resource flexibility across the business. The structure also delivers benefits for legal team members, who are able to expand their skillsets without losing their areas of specialization, and to work in squads to learn entirely new areas of practice. Agile has a bottom-line impact, too; working as Agile teams creates a more adaptive and responsive organization, speeding up the product lifecycle and getting products to market more quickly (an important differentiator for the TMT sector in particular). Once the organizational model has been transformed, the foundations are successfully laid to bring in technology to support the new ways of working.

Creating a digital-first legal function

Another member at the Digital Legal Exchange is leading the legal team at a fast-growing data company. Unlike many of our members, who are dealing with legacy technologies and entrenched ways of working, because the member is a scale-up, the corporate legal team has been designed as a digital-first greenfield organization. Processes have been developed to enable digital delivery and systems and technologies have been identified and implemented to support the delivery model. The member's legal team implemented the following technologies within the first year of operations:

- A configurable CLM tool, with templates, third party agreements, authorization matrix, and approval mechanisms.
- Integration with an e-signature tool as part of the end-to-end contract workflow.
- A ticketing system for the legal team to provide support to internal clients (this also acts as a knowledge system – new legal team members can see how tickets/requests have been resolved in the past).
- A chatbot for first line legal support built into Slack, the business' internal communications tool.
- A searchable repository for all enterprise agreements.

According to the Exchange member, the business benefits of this greenfield digital approach are significant. The legal team is highly motivated and is able to focus on delivering higher-value legal work. Customer satisfaction levels are extremely high, as the legal team is able to anticipate business needs and to identify and solve issues before they become problematic.

Creating a "digital legal front door"

An Exchange member in the financial services sector has successfully implemented a "digital legal front door" – a digital channel/platform between (internal) clients and the corporate legal department, on which legal services are delivered. The digital front door gives internal clients access to digitalized legal services without the need to contact individual lawyers via telephone or email. Far from detracting from the service to internal customers, the platform delivers a superior client experience, and also functions as a repository for the team's legal know-how. The digital front door allows for dynamic resource allocation and smart routing of legal requests to expert teams or centers of excellence – and collects data that can be used to improve delivery over time. Other use cases for a digital front door include:

- Self-service and semi self-service: semi self-service is a subset of self-service in which the internal client completes up to 80 percent of a task, then routes the task to the lawyer to finalize, who then sends the completed task to the client.

- Document/contract assembly or pre-assembly: allowing an internal client to access contract clauses to automate the generation of a contract.
- Corporate legal department internal know-how distribution: using the platform to share know-how inside the legal department. Some legal teams are reluctant to share information; the digital legal front door can help to change this behavior and encourage sharing. It can also act as a form of internal "LinkedIn" for legal expertise, giving other lawyers visibility of the skills, experience, and capabilities of other legal team members.

In terms of business benefit, the digital legal front door liberates lawyers from mundane or non-strategic tasks, and frees up capacity for the legal department to work on the more strategically important questions, and issues of long term, material legal risk.

Developing and commercializing legal products

Legal know-how can itself be a direct source of value for the business. Legal functions have begun to recognize the potential in "productizing" their knowledge and commercializing it in the market. The corporate legal team of an Exchange member in the financial services sector has developed and white-labelled a product which contains templates to operationalize a financial services regulation in a particular jurisdiction. This product will be sold to smaller, non-competitive organizations in the same sector operating in the same jurisdiction. In terms of business benefits, the product will generate a small revenue stream, but this is not the primary driver. The initiative is as much about cultural change as it is about revenue generation. For the legal department, so often cast as the business blocker, there is immeasurable cultural value in demonstrating that the lawyers' sophisticated legal advice has a market value.

Using data to demonstrate value

The legal department has a unique advantage, as its reach runs horizontally across the entire business. Consequently, the data that flows through legal is not simply "legal data", to be used to make the legal function more efficient. It is enterprise data that can give a deep insight into how the wider business is performing. At the Exchange, a number of our members are recognizing the potential of leveraging enterprise data that flows through the legal function to demonstrate value to the business:

- One member, who leads the litigation and disputes team in a global technology company, is using the data to which legal has access to identify areas for improvement in particular business units. The legal team has a KPI layer on top of this data to allow it to demonstrate, from a P&L standpoint, how the legal function has contributed to business success.
- Another member proactively analyses data in commercial contracts to identify revenue opportunities for the sales team (e.g., auto-renewal clauses or opportunities for price increases).
- Another member, whose organization has a large number of employees globally, uses legal data to generate a report showing the frequency of labor claims by location, allowing for a root cause analysis that can be presented to the business.

Final thoughts

These are a few, selected examples of Exchange members that are using technology as part of a wider digital transformation effort to support a re-imagined legal service delivery model. These examples of best practice reinforce the core principles of a successful digital transformation:

- Technology should enable, not lead, the transformation. Technology is only one part of the picture, to be introduced after underlying processes and the service delivery model have themselves been transformed.
- Technology should enable better customer service. The objective of any technology implementation is to make the legal function more adaptive and responsive to the business, and to narrow the legal/business disconnect.
- Technology should support the strategy. Any technology must be introduced to support the wider strategic aims of the enterprise, rather than to solve individual problems.

As the momentum for legal digital transformation continues to build, it is our hope that these examples of best practice will help other corporate legal functions to shape their strategies with confidence. To find out more about our work at the Digital Legal Exchange, visit www.dlex.org.

References

1 John P. Kotter *et al*, *Change: How organizations achieve hard-to-imagine results in uncertain and volatile times*, 2021, John Wiley & Sons, Inc.
2 Michele DeStefano, Bjarne P. Tellmann & Daniel Wu. February 2022. *Don't Let the Digital Tail Wag the Transformation Dog: A Digital Transformation Roadmap for Corporate Counsel*, p.16. SSRN https://papers.ssrn.com/sol3/papers.cfm?abstract_id=4021593.
3 www.mckinsey.com/business-functions/strategy-and-corporate-finance/our-insights/how-covid-19-has-pushed-companies-over-the-technology-tipping-point-and-transformed-business-forever
4 www.ey.com/en_gr/law/general-counsel-imperative-barriers-building-blocks
5 Michele DeStefano, Bjarne P. Tellmann & Daniel Wu. February 2022. *Don't Let the Digital Tail Wag the Transformation Dog: A Digital Transformation Roadmap for Corporate Counsel*, p.16. SSRN https://papers.ssrn.com/sol3/papers.cfm?abstract_id=4021593.
6 *Ibid*, p.19.
7 *Ibid*, p.23.
8 *Ibid*, p.16.
9 *Ibid*, p.8.
10 Michael Bucy, Bill Schaninger, Kate VanAkin, Brooke Weddle, *Losing from day one: Why even successful transformations fall short*, December 2021, McKinsey & Company. www.mckinsey.com/business-functions/people-and-organizational-performance/our-insights/successful-transformations
11 *Ibid*.
12 Jim Murphy *et al*, *Predicts 2021: Corporate Legal and Compliance Technology*, 25 November 2020, Gartner, Inc.

Chapter 7: Considerations on doing more with less – leading the lean legal department

By Maja Fabula, vice president and deputy general counsel, Tenneco Inc.

Introduction

As in-house counsel for a global manufacturing company, I have visited manufacturing plants around the world. One thing that struck me was that several plants had a similar sign: "STOP… CALL… WAIT". This sign is an important safety reminder. If an operator experiences a problem on the production line, the operator should STOP, preventing the problem from growing. The operator then CALLS for help and WAITS. Production does not resume until the problem is resolved.

These signs struck a chord for me because the day-to-day work of a lean legal team can feel the opposite. We move quickly between meetings. We field questions from business colleagues about a variety of topics. We face competing deadlines, often putting work aside when a more pressing issue arises. Even as we juggle all inbound requests, we must stay ahead of emerging legal issues.

When I first began drafting this chapter, I focused on the juggling. There are several different tactics leaders can use to match demand for legal services against available resources. However, as I thought through this topic, I realized that I was skipping a step. I had fallen into the trap of assuming every inbound question a legal team receives should be handled. Starting with that mindset risks making a lean team even thinner.

So, I begin this chapter with the premise that doing "more with less" does not mean doing *everything*. In a lean environment, a leader must stop and understand the full range of legal challenges facing the business and prioritize them accordingly. From that point of departure, you can help your team members identify the higher priority work and enlist support from business partners along the way.

Next, this chapter discusses the importance of focusing on your team's wellbeing as you navigate lean times. At a personal level, I believe that supporting your team members is one of the most important responsibilities of a leader. As a practical matter, your team's understanding of the business, legal expertise, and engagement are the most valuable resources the legal department has. Working with your team to deploy their talents more effectively helps you use lean resources most effectively.

Finally, this chapter closes by suggesting a few tactics to take work out of the system. I recognize that every legal department operates differently. I hope these suggestions spark your thinking about what is possible. Because we are all juggling, every day. Even small changes to make a team's workload more manageable can help your legal team be more productive and engaged.

Doing more with less – the importance of prioritization

In this chapter, I refer often to having a "lean" team. Lean originated in the manufacturing industry as an operational model focused on driving efficiency and reducing waste.[1] The concept of being lean has proliferated to staffing models, management practices, and business philosophies. Regardless of context, lean practices share a common focus – ensuring that resources are used in the most effective and efficient way possible. Consequently, whether by design or by default, in a lean environment, extra resources are unavailable.[2] Consequently, when new demand arises, you must figure out how to do more with less.

In this respect, a lean legal team does not give equal attention to all matters. Instead, a lean team makes dozens of decisions each week about who will handle a request, how much time that project will receive, and when the necessary work will be completed. All too often, this prioritization is driven by demand. The business partners who make the most (or loudest) requests for legal advice receive the most attention. Projects marked "urgent" consume the most resources. As a leader, you must see past the noise and define the department's priorities.

Fortunately, the legal team is uniquely positioned to prioritize its work assignments. A legal team routinely connects with both business partners and other corporate functions. Legal also works with management and the board on business strategy, risk management, compliance, and regulatory developments. In short, the legal team's network spans the breadth of the company.

This broad perspective provides a powerful starting point for prioritizing your legal team's work. You can see which legal matters are more impactful for the business. As a lawyer, you can also assess the risks the company is facing. Indeed, one of the jobs of an in-house lawyer is to "see around corners" and be proactive. These two elements – the strategic importance of the legal work your team performs *and* your assessment of legal risk – should be the starting point of how you prioritize work and allocate resources.

For example, imagine a business unit that is tasked with growing top line revenue by seven percent annually. One commercial lead has identified a new potential market segment and is sending the legal team many new business proposals and contracts for review. This business partner is quickly consuming resources, all in support of the objective of top-line growth.

At first glance, this business partner's requests would seem to require prioritization. After all, this commercial initiative has the potential to capture new revenue. However, the legal team should pause before diving into the project to evaluate how this commercial work fits into the business unit's overall strategy. How important is capturing business from a new market segment vs growing the existing customer base? Does the business case include the regulatory requirements for this new market segment? How does this project compare to other initiatives to increase top-line revenue? Without this understanding, the legal team cannot triage its work effectively. Instead, the team will be in an uncomfortable position of trying to respond to requests that may not actually further the business unit's overall strategy.

Scale this approach across your team

Efforts to prioritize work are most effective when all members of the legal team have a shared understanding of why certain work is a priority and speak with "one voice" to their business partners. This enables your contributors to understand the reasons for the work they are being asked to prioritize. They can spend time addressing critical projects, rather than reacting to inbound demands.

There are many ways to communicate this approach to your broader legal team. Some in-house teams rely on regular meetings or weekly reports for communication of key matters. Other departments have invested in electronic tools that allow managers to identify critical matters and route work accordingly. Regardless of the process you select, the objective is a wholistic view of the work being performed so you can drive prioritization across those projects.

Once you open the door to this approach, a conversation should develop between department managers and team members about their workload. This conversation is not intended to focus on the day-to-day progress of matters. Rather, ask your team members to share their view on the volume of work they are facing and the strategic importance of, and risks posed by, their different matters. These discussions provide a valuable opportunity for the leaders to "pulse check" where their teams are focusing and redirect, as appropriate. Moreover, having these discussions as a team (versus one-to-one) supports a consistent prioritization across the legal team.

Create a feedback loop with business partners

What I have described above is a very inward-looking approach to define priorities for the legal department. The benefit of this approach is amplified if you can secure the support of your business partners. One way to do that is to "speak the language" of the business.

Each member of the legal team must understand the objectives of their business partners and how those objectives are measured.[3] This knowledge can be gained in many ways – i.e., participating in an operations review, touring an engineering center, or attending a product presentation. Such experiences can provide meaningful insight on the operations of the company and create connections with key members of the business teams. These touchpoints also provide opportunities for the lawyers to ask how legal can best support the business.

To maintain this engagement between business and the legal team, set the expectation that your team members have regular check-ins with their business partners. These discussions enable lawyers to stay current as business objectives shift. In exchange, the legal team should update the business partners on the types of requests and legal issues being raised. Lawyers should be transparent about how projects were being prioritized and welcome feedback on whether that prioritization was consistent with the objectives of the business. Without this collaboration, business partners will see legal as mercurial – quick to act on some requests, while others are placed on the back burner. Creating a feedback loop avoids this outcome because it enables business and legal to share knowledge and agree on an approach to managing competing priorities.

Your legal team's wellbeing is a critical priority

In a lean environment, it is natural for leaders to focus on efficiency and productivity. After all, when resources are limited, it is important to ensure they are being used effectively. Likewise, legal teams will always be called upon to optimize their limited budgets. However, being an effective leader of a lean team requires looking beyond the numbers and prioritizing your team's wellbeing.

I suggest a focus on wellbeing for a few reasons. First, a lean team is always under pressure and has higher burn-out risk. I believe managers must be responsible for finding ways to reduce that pressure and for helping their team members manage through stressful times. If you are not paying attention to your team's wellbeing, you will miss important signs that they are overwhelmed, making them less effective. This will feed a downward spiral of frustration, decreasing morale, and poor performance.

Second, wellbeing is a key driver of engagement which, in turn, drives retention.[4] Retention is of critical importance for a lean team. An in-house legal team has unique knowledge of how business works, gained through years of experience. While outside counsel can supply legal expertise, they cannot provide an in-house lawyer's ability to solve problems and navigate the organization. Consequently, when a team member leaves the legal department, a knowledge gap opens that can take months (if not years) to fill.[5] Focusing on the wellbeing of your team also increases the company's ability to retain key talent.

Finally, even in an environment of limited resources, you can influence wellbeing. I've suggested a few ideas below. What I hope stands out is that these are actions you can take with little cash outlay. Instead, what they require is focused attention and thoughtfulness.

Set the tone for your team – their wellbeing matters

Fostering wellbeing starts with the expectations we set as leaders. I say this because a lean team will always have more work than it can reasonably complete. In that respect, consider what you are communicating to your team – i.e., what expectations you are setting – about the backlog of assignments that are delayed or incomplete. This is not an easy question to answer. It requires considering whether your team member is prioritizing effectively, whether there are performance issues, or whether the workload is simply too much for one person. How you approach this question will set the tone for your team. I want to offer two examples from my own experience to help you navigate this question.

First, I noticed my team had developed a vacation problem. Team members responded to emails promptly and joined conference calls when they were supposed to be on the beach. When you asked someone "How was your vacation?" the response inevitably included mention of how much they worked. This behavior prevents people from getting a break from work and normalizes working during vacations. If unchecked, working during vacation contributes to dissatisfaction and turnover.[6]

I decided to tackle this concern head-on. My goal was to communicate that personal time was as valuable as productivity and to back that commitment with action. I empowered team members to step away by setting an objective process for coordinating vacation coverage.[7] I also shared my vacation schedule and asked my team to attend meetings or cover matters in my absence. As the process became engrained, team members began stepping in to help each other cover matters without being asked.

As a second example, during the initial wave of the COVID-19 pandemic, our legal team was called upon to advise on an overwhelming quantity of new issues.[8] We worked nights and through weekends, trying to stay ahead of rapidly-changing regulations and an extremely dynamic business environment. When facing this type of crisis, it seems as though the work will never end. Which is why it is so important to stop and consider how you, as a manager, expect your team to respond to the pressure. The direction you give sets the tone for the team.

Accordingly, during the first months of the COVID-19 pandemic, I focused on eliminating duplicative work and freeing up time for lawyers to focus on key matters. To reduce duplication of effort, I tracked the issues each lawyer was facing and then consolidated work product where all could access it. I also summarized key issues, and new resources available, in an end-of-the-day update message so team members would have resources readily available. Finally, I blocked calendars on Friday afternoons to reserve time to close out key tasks and permit a respite at the end of a hard week. The expectation was set that we would all contribute to supporting our company, and each other, through this unique time, and no one would work until the edge of burn-out. Our legal department ultimately came out of the pandemic as a stronger team.

Identifying drivers of wellbeing

When trying to decide how to support your team's wellbeing, I encourage you to ask them. In a recent article from the *Harvard Business Review*,[9] Marcus Buckingham suggests a few questions to start this conversation and better understand what drives members of your team. Borrowing from his suggestions, I incorporated a few open-ended questions into my standing team meetings:

- What went well this week? And what didn't?
- What are your priorities this coming week? How can I best help?
- What did you want to do, but weren't able to get to?

These basic questions sparked conversations about how my team perceived their contributions to the company. They were also able to raise any pain points for us to troubleshoot together. I thus gained new insights into how they viewed their role as legal advisor and what aspects of that role provided the most satisfaction.

For example, one lawyer mentioned that he was feeling stuck on what he described as a "small issue". He was receiving many requests from his business partners for non-disclosure agreements (NDAs) for new projects. Instead of directing requestors to the company's online widget for generating NDAs, this lawyer was handling all the drafting himself, thinking that NDAs were relatively simple and easy for him to complete. What started with good intentions – a desire to be a responsive, collaborative business partner – had the unintended effect of deterring our business partners from using a valuable online tool. In the end, while the actual time required by these NDAs was only a few hours a week, they were a drain on this lawyer's energy and focus. Our conversation provided an opportunity to discuss the priorities of the business, ultimately empowering him to say no to these NDA requests. These conversations may also identify opportunities for your team members to do more of what they most enjoy. In this respect, you may need to let go of the traditional lean viewpoint that eschews inefficiencies and waste. After all, the person taking on the challenge will need to spend (non-productive) time learning. And you'll need to find someone else to complete the work left behind. The counterpoint, though, is that providing new areas of responsibility is a tremendous development tool and driver of engagement. These qualitative gains must be balanced against the costs of introducing inefficiency. You may find that your commitment to supporting your team in this way pays unexpected dividends in developing a higher level of expertise and driving engagement, retention, and wellbeing.

Maximizing resources in a lean environment – removing work from the system

Establishing priorities (and communicating them to your team) is the first step in increasing the effectiveness of a lean team. The second step requires finding ways to make those priorities real. This can be the hardest part. After all, no lawyer wants to turn away business partners with the message their requests are not important. I suggest below a few methods to reduce demand on your lawyers, while still meeting business needs. The objective of these different processes is the same – taking work out of the system to give your lawyers the time to focus on the most critical tasks.

Using scorecards for workflow management

Using a scorecard to screen requests for legal support can be an effective way to manage demand. In its simplest form, a scorecard assigns points for new requests based on risk, urgency, and strategic importance. Projects are then routed for review, depending on the score they receive. A scorecard thus introduces objectivity and predictability into the process of workflow management.

Creating a scorecard requires an understanding of the work being performed and its strategic significance to the business. My colleague and in-house lawyer, Adam Kochenderfer, developed standardized workflows for commercial contract reviews and summarized his approach succinctly:

> *"You may have a hammer, but not every problem is a nail. Effective, lean legal departments pair appropriate resources with tasks. This requires thoughtful consideration of relative risks, business priorities, and the full toolbox available to modern-day counsel."*

Putting this theory into practice requires an objective mapping of the work your team is handling and the commonalities within these assignments. To illustrate a few steps:

1. *Define the scope.* Identify tasks with elements in common that reoccur on a regular basis. The volume and frequency of this work must be high enough to warrant the investment to build a scorecard and to yield efficiency gains.
2. *Identify the variables you will measure.* Focusing on the elements in common within this group of tasks, identify the discrete variables that are indicative of risk, and that can be answered yes/no or with a quantitative variable, i.e., Does the project relate to a critical business objective? How much revenue is at stake? Does the project involve legal issues the company has identified as high-risk?
3. *Assign a points scale.* Once you have identified the variables you will evaluate, you must decide how to assign points to the potential outcomes of each variable. These points then add up to a score, which drives the prioritization of the task.
4. *Refine your weighting.* Review the weighting of your proposed point scale with your business partners, providing examples of how recent projects would be handled under this new scorecard. This discussion should be collaborative, not adversarial. It is ultimately a joint effort to ensure that most critical matters receive the timeliest attention.
5. *Define workflow paths.* The score the project receives drives how the project is handled by the legal team. A low-scoring project may receive a red flag review by a paralegal, or contract manager, following a pre-defined checklist. By contrast, a high-scoring project will receive focused attention from a subject matter specialist or in-house lawyer.

This scorecard challenges the assumption that every project requires equal attention. It also empowers lawyers to reduce the time spent on lower-value work. Once the process becomes engrained, it channels lawyers' attention and expertise to projects where they will have the greatest impact.

Scaling knowledge to reduce demand

In-house lawyers frequently experience *déjà vu* – despite best efforts, questions we address inevitably resurface in the future. For example, an employment lawyer will receive similar questions from several different human resources managers. A litigation lawyer will be asked repeatedly when a legal hold is required and how to implement it. While understandable, this phenomenon squanders resources and erodes the morale of lawyers who may feel their advice is being ignored.

For a lean law department, a matter management database that preserves work product and knowledge may be out of reach. Even so, it is still possible to scale knowledge to reduce demand. The first step to doing so is identifying the questions that are repeating. I encourage lawyers to keep a deskside tally of the issues being raised by their business partners. Likewise, legal department managers should stay alert for team members expressing frustration that their advice is repeatedly falling on deaf ears.

Once you have identified recurring issues, the lawyer must find a way to package the advice in a way that is accessible for future use. A lawyer must "make the effort"[10] to articulate the knowledge and capture it in writing. An easy option is developing short FAQs or a process checklist for key topics. Similarly, outside counsel can be asked to convert their feedback into a one-page summary in bullet point format. This simple repackaging allows advice to be preserved, as compared to emails which are easily lost in crowded in-boxes. Whatever format you choose, documenting responses to recurring questions should not be time-consuming. Instead, approach this task with the mindset that spending more time upfront to preserve the feedback will reduce work in the future.

You can progress this approach by proactively communicating, instead of waiting for the repeat question to resurface. I'd like to share an example that was the inspiration of in-house employment lawyers. These lawyers frequently fielded questions from human resources personnel and identified several topics that were coming up over and over. They teamed up to hold a weekly forum and invited their primary contacts from human resources. During this meeting, the lawyers reviewed the "hot topic" of the week and then opened the floor for questions. Human resources team members began suggesting topics for discussion and expanded participation across the group. What began as an effort to reduce the number of repeat questions evolved into a venue to share knowledge and learn from each other.

Accelerate your new team members (and outside counsel)

I would like to ask you to pause for a minute and remember your first in-house counsel position. Whether you joined a corporation from a law firm, government, or immediately after graduation, you had to learn how to navigate a new environment. Think of the questions you had, which likely ranged from "How do I file an expense report?" and "Where are contracts saved?" to "Who needs to approve this transaction?" and "How do we ensure covenant compliance?" Now, put yourself in the shoes of a new lawyer joining your team. How will this information be shared with them? More importantly, what can you do to accelerate their integration into the team?

When I first began building my team, I asked these questions and identified a short checklist of must-know points for new hires. I then built a curriculum around those points. It has evolved over the years, but the key components remain the same: (i) a series of meetings with members of the legal team to introduce the new hire to key department processes and databases; (ii) new hires are matched with an internal colleague to serve as informal mentor; and (iii) all new hires receive a Company 101 training presentation.

The Company 101 training has had the largest impact because it provides context to the matters the new hire will address. The presentation covers the basics of how the company's business segments are organized, strategic objectives of each product line, and key personnel within each business. It also includes information about the company's legal structure and relevant corporate history. This training, and onboarding program, enables new team members to become more effective, sooner. It also eliminates the time new hires will spend chasing down answers to basic questions.

A Company 101 training can also be shared with your company's outside lawyers. Outside lawyers who are handling fact-intensive matters – such as litigation, due diligence, and commercial negotiations – will benefit from a deeper understanding of their client's operations, corporate structure, and business priorities. Providing this knowledge early in the engagement builds a framework for outside counsel to be better, more efficient, advocates for your business.

Taking your first step

This chapter has described a few tactics for managing demand in a lean environment. While I wish I could provide a roadmap for implementing the ideas I think are most impactful, I recognize that every organization and legal department is different. When resources are constrained, taking on additional work to do more with less can seem daunting. So, if I could offer one final suggestion, it would be to consider whether the current operating model of your team, lean or otherwise, is sustainable for the long term. That is, consider what will happen if you do not act. Will you be able to retain your key contributors? Can your team continue to provide effective, actionable advice to their business partners? Do your culture and working environment support, or detract from, your team's wellbeing?

Once you have found the area you would like to focus on, take one step forward. A single, sustainable change, even if small, can have a tremendous impact in the long run. And, most importantly, you will be demonstrating to your team and business partners that you understand the demands they are facing and are prepared to support them through lean times.

References

1 Lean manufacturing deploys a system (pioneered by Toyota) that drives efficiency through rigorous process management, attention to detail, and data-driven approaches. See Bradley Staats and David Upton, *Lean Knowledge Work*, Harvard Business Review (October 2011).

2 Lean staffing also has a negative association, i.e., that resources are not sufficient for the task at hand: "The goal is typically to have just enough workers to cover demand, and no more, leaving little margin for error." See David Yaffe-Bellamy and Noam Schreiber, *Starbucks' Gathering Spot Model is Threatened by Coronavirus*, *NY Times* (12 March 2020), www.nytimes.com/2020/03/12/business/starbucks-coronavirus.html.

3 I also encourage team members to "speak the language" literally. When I first became an in-house counsel, I was surprised by the extent of internal shorthand. Every business unit I encountered seemed to have its own set of acronyms and abbreviations. So, when our legal team began growing, we equipped new hires with a glossary of these terms and a who's who list to help them navigate the company.

4 Gallup, *What is Employee Engagement and How Do You Improve It*, available at www.gallup.com/workplace/285674/improve-employee-engagement-workplace.aspx#ite-357458 (last visited 20 August 2022) ("Engaged employees produce better business outcomes than other employees – across industry, company size and nationality, and in good economic times and bad"); see further, SHRM, *Toolkit for Developing and Sustaining Employee Engagement*, available at www.shrm.org/

resourcesandtools/tools-and-samples/toolkits/pages/sustainingemployeeengagement.aspx (last visited 15 August 2022) ("Not only does engagement have the potential to significantly affect employee retention, productivity and loyalty, it is also a key link to customer satisfaction, company reputation and overall stakeholder value.").

5 Major, Lindsey & Africa, a leading legal recruiting firm (www.mlaglobal.com), advises clients that generally, the time frame to back-fill/add a member to an in-house legal team ranges from four to six months. However, they highlight that many factors can easily extend this stated time frame. These factors can include, but are not limited to (a) the parameters of the search (required practice area expertise and/or industry expertise); (b) the seniority level of the search (GC/CLO level or supporting level and reporting structure); (c) the attractiveness of the company (continued growth, expansion, stability); (d) the location for the role (metropolitan area, suburb); (e) the need for relocation of a candidate (and family); (f) return to work policy; and (g) bonus payments and stock vesting schedules of prior employer.

6 See Kathryn Tyler, *A Nation in Need of a Vacation*, 17 July 2021, available at www.shrm.org/hr-today/news/all-things-work/pages/a-nation-in-need-of-a-vacation.aspx (last visited 19 August 2022) (discussing impact of vacation time on retention productivity and morale) and Laurel Kasler, *Employees who Work on Vacation are More Likely to Quit*, 29 July 2022 available at www.hrdive.com/news/employees-who-work-on-vacation-are-more-likely-to-quit-survey-finds/628243/ (last visited 19 August 2022) (reporting results of survey of 1,000 employees).

7 The process was straightforward. At least one week before going on vacation, team members would review a list of open projects with their manager to identify what needed coverage. The team member was responsible for preparing the matter for hand-off and the manager was responsible for supervising a smooth transition.

8 Indeed, the last few years have been particularly challenging, as corporate law departments are facing an increase in workload, without corresponding increase in budget. See, Thompson Reuters, *State of Corporate Legal Departments 2022* and *State of Corporate Legal Departments 2021*, available at: www.thomsonreuters.com/en-us/posts/legal/state-of-corporate-law-departments-2022/.

9 https://hbr.org/2022/05/designing-work-that-people-love

10 See Bradley Staats and David Upton, *Lean Knowledge Work*, Harvard Business Review (October 2011) (explaining application of lean principles to 'knowledge work': "For one thing, a substantial amount of knowledge assumed to be tacit doesn't have to be; it can be articulated and captured in writing if the organization makes the effort to pull it out of people's heads.").

Chapter 8: Crisis prevention and management – how must legal and communications act together?

By Christian Lawrence, partner, Brunswick Group

Introduction

Sooner or later, every company encounters a crisis that can threaten its reputation. It would be a victory of the principle of hope over the principle of experience to be able to go about one's business without internal or external disruption. Even a glance at the business section of the daily press shows the many corners from which mostly negative surprises can affect the respective business model. Apart from cases of clear breach of duty, corporate managements tend to externalize responsibility for the respective triggers of the problem, be it in relation to scarce supplies (semiconductors), geopolitical upheavals (Ukraine conflict), or the general financial crisis (most recently in 2008), to name but a few. One is quickly tempted to speak of the "black swan" that supposedly no one could have foreseen. But sometimes the crisis is rather the result of poor risk management, convenient looking the other way and a failure to prepare.[1]

A "golden truism" to begin with – the best crisis management starts before the crisis has occurred and is characterized by a comprehensive view of the risk landscape by assessing and prioritizing risks in terms of their probability of occurrence and the respective extent of damage. At the operational level, this is the responsibility of the respective chief risk officer of the company. But for the management of the impact of corporate decisions on the company's reputation, it is precisely the good cooperation between the legal and communications departments that is of great importance. Both departments can increase resilience to critical developments, not only in a crisis, but also during normal operations. Together, they can take precautions that minimize the occurrence of fundamental differences of opinion and dangerous role conflicts at the moment of crisis, when rapid and coordinated action is required. This is very important, if only because almost every corporate crisis has legal implications. These may not only be claims for damages by customers or shareholders. Claims by an "activist" shareholder, investigations by government authorities, or the question of how to deal with the duty of care for employees accused of serious misconduct with a negative impact on the company's reputation are also examples of the diversity of critical disputes with stakeholders, regardless of whether they are in the right or not. The classic conflict is as follows – a problem has become known, the waves of excitement run high on social media, explanations and consequences are demanded. In many such cases, it is completely unclear what happened in the first place.

Typically, the legal department does not want to see anything communicated in such a situation, while the "golden rule" of corporate communications dictates exactly the opposite; show concern, provide explanations, enable classifications ("How could this happen?"). The problem is made more difficult by the fact that external "accusers" (journalists, influencers) make allegations, investors ask questions, the share price is under pressure. Exaggeratedly, the latent clash of interests between the legal and communications sectors is described as a "*conflict between offensive storytelling and technocratic defense*".[2] Not infrequently, there are disputes, valuable time is lost, and a CEO who is also often overburdened has to make decisions. In case of doubt, mistakes happen. Because each case is different, it is not possible to give any schematic hints in advance. There is positive experience of cooperation in so-called "litigation PR", where one's own legal position is publicly explained during court proceedings and the arguments of the opposing party are shaken by PR measures.[3] But how can the cooperation be optimized in the stages before, especially in the crucial moment when the crisis becomes known for the first time?

Reputation and trust as assets

"Reputation" corresponds to the perception of a company's factual competence and action-related integrity. "Stakeholders" are those who directly or indirectly influence the company. The most important ones are customers, shareholders, employees, and the general public. A company's reputation among these stakeholders determines whether its products are purchased, whether people invest in its stock, or whether it is chosen as an employer. Important intermediaries in shaping opinion are financial and environmental rating agencies, associations, the media, and regulators. Consensus with and acceptance by non-governmental organizations (NGOs) are all the more relevant the greater the interface of a company with socially discussed framework conditions, especially with regard to environmental issues.

Reputational crises usually also have a direct impact on the share price.

This is, among others, one of the reasons why many companies measure their reputation on the basis of defined and communicated parameters and regularly report on this in their annual reports.[4] In recent years, the good reputation of numerous companies has suffered greatly as a result of scandals. Violations of compliance rules, product defects, environmental pollution, or simply the insensitive handling of customers' legitimate interests have often been the trigger for a disruption of a company's lasting relationship with its stakeholders. In quite a few cases, the reputation-damaging effect also radiates to other industry participants, even though they themselves did not engage in the originally incriminated behavior. The banking industry in the aftermath of the 2008 financial crisis can be cited as an example.

Which issues give rise to the greatest reputational risks for companies? This question is not easy to answer, because it depends heavily on how society as a whole views certain issues. However, indications are provided by the annual Allianz survey of risk managers (most recent 2022), which names the following topics as the most important primary risks.[5]

The most important global business risks for 2022. Source: Allianz Global Corporate & Speciality

How quickly such prioritizations can change is shown by Russia's war of aggression on Ukraine in February 2022, which abruptly led to a discussion about geopolitical conflict risks, the security of supply of critical goods such as grain, or the consideration of the defense industry from an ESG perspective, to name just the most important aspects.

At the core of reputation is "Trust", understood as the consequence of fulfilled promises, predictions that come true and values that one lives by.[6] A good indicator of trust is the annual *Edelman Trust Barometer*, which is a representative survey of which institutions (government/media/business/NGOs) are considered by the population to be competent to solve current problems.[7] Trust in the corporate context, as in politics, is a personal rather than an institutional component. It is based on people who are either respected professionally and personally or not. For example, when you think of J.P. Morgan, you think of CEO Jamie Dimon. Berkshire Hathaway is associated with Warren Buffett, Tesla with Elon Musk. If the chief corporate communication officer fails to present the CEO and as many of the other board members as possible in the defined set of opinion-leading media, he or she misses a vital opportunity to build trust. After all, in the event of a crisis, it is these people who can provide assessments and evaluations which, depending on one's own set of values, one may or may not find correct. In this way, with a clever approach, the CEO can even be positioned as the "arbiter" of a problem in the company he or she leads, although strictly speaking he/she is thereby evaluating his/her own task.

The crisis as a threat – and an opportunity

A crisis is the sudden deterioration of public perception with the risk of permanent damage to reputation and trust. As a result, there is a threat of a change in behavior on the part of customers, investors, employees, and the rest of the public. Crises are of a very different and predominantly unpredictable nature. The Volkswagen issue, Enron, and the abuse scandals of the Catholic Church are still well anchored in the collective memory. Some of these crises disappear just as quickly as they emerged, while others dominate the headlines for weeks or months and become firmly entrenched in public perception.

For example, while oil tankers continue to crash on the world's oceans today, when asked unsupported for an example case, the *Exxon Valdez* accident in Alaska, more than 30 years ago, is regularly cited. Other accidents and scandals, on the other hand, are not visible, take place completely in the shadows, or do not take root in the collective memory, despite being dutifully mentioned in the media. Examples of these include the *Tylenol* problem (Johnson & Johnson) or the case of the "stuck accelerator pedal" (Toyota), which are generally regarded as examples of very good crisis management.

So what determines whether a crisis has an effect that threatens the company's existence, or whether it is shelved by the media after a short period of consideration? The answer lies in the way the company in question deals with the problem. In the face of enormous performance compression and high return expectations, the public has accepted that companies make mistakes. But it does not accept when the mistake is handled irresponsibly; the arbiter of this is not the company, but public opinion. So it is important, especially at the beginning of a crisis, to show public sympathy for those who have been harmed and to avoid any kind of self-centeredness.

Typical triggers of crises can be as follows.

Man-made accidents and natural disasters:

- Environmental pollution caused by oil production in Nigeria (Shell).
- The sinking of the *Exxon Valdez* (Exxon).
- The accident of the *Costa Concordia* (Costa Crociere).
- The suicide of the co-pilot of the Germanwings flight 9525 (Lufthansa).
- The attacks of September 11, 2001 (various insurers).
- The blockade of the Suez Canal due to the accident of the *Ever Given* with worldwide disruption of logistics chains (Evergreen Marine).
- The rupture of the tailings dam in Brumadinho/Brazil (Vale).

External macroeconomic circumstances:

- Semiconductor crisis.
- Russia sanctions.
- Low interest rate environment/inflation.
- Cyberattack.
- Pandemic-related staff shortages.

Corporate crisis:

- Poor risk management.
- Compliance incidents (Libor scandals).
- Strategy breach, unethical behavior, fraud at the top (Wirecard, Enron).
- Insider breach, conflicts between boards, missed targets/profit warning, offensive advertising (J&J "whitening cream", Volkswagen).
- Dissonance with societal demands.

Product defects/recalls:

- Takata Air Bag.
- Volkswagen Diesel.
- Samsung Galaxy Note 7 phone.

HR crisis:

- Succession issues.
- Death of key personnel.

Each crisis is different, develops differently, and is usually difficult to predict. However, there are criteria that have a significant impact on the intensity of the perception of a crisis in the formation of public opinion.

The topic

Certain issues catch the public imagination more than others. As a rule of thumb, surprising issues that contrast with the company's traditional value proposition while also interfering with people's personal lives are more dangerous than issues where everyone says "That suits the originator" or "This has nothing to do with me personally". These tend to have a lower potential for excitement. One example is the Wells Fargo scandal (2016), in which the bank, which is considered customer-focused and reputable, opened over two million fake accounts to fake sales and increase employee bonuses.

"David vs Goliath"

The audience's sympathy is intuitively with the weaker, the one with whom the viewer themselves can most easily identify. A good example of this problem was Greenpeace vs Shell in 1995, where Greenpeace argued against the sinking of an oil rig (Brent Spar) with false environmental data. Afterwards, it turned out that the sinking would have been the more environmentally friendly measure, for which Greenpeace apologized. Greenpeace was much less resourced then than it is now. The mechanism also worked in the lawsuits of the Deutsche Umwelthilfe (DUH) against large corporations such as Volkswagen.

Framing

Framing means presenting information in a context that distracts the target group from a negative connotation and transforms it into a positive perception. Are pesticides "poison" on the plate, or necessary to give a growing world population access to affordable food? To focus on a very practical example, a PR person writing a press release about ground beef would probably write that the product is "75 percent low fat" rather than "it is 25 percent fat".

History of similar incidents

If there have been similar incidents before, the intuitive accusation is "You have learned nothing from the past". The most recent example is the abuse scandals in the Catholic Church, where the impression is created that those responsible, despite decades of knowledge of the incidents, did not take sufficient precautions against further repetitions.

Interconnection of the tasks of the legal department and the communications department

Companies must take precautions to prevent incidents damaging their reputation and, should they occur, to limit such damage. In essence, the legal department defends the company's legal position in the legal drafting phase and, in the case of contentious disputes, in the pre-litigation and litigation phase. And it is precisely here that cooperation between the communications and legal departments of a company, which often report to different members of the board (Communications typically to the CEO, legal mostly to the CFO), plays an important role. Ideally, the two functions can complement each other, but in cases that are unfortunately frequently encountered, conflicts arise that can have an inhibiting effect on the swift management of a crisis and, as a result alone, give the impression that the company is "cold-hearted" or "intransigent", an impression that is difficult to correct.

Corporate communications represents the company's concerns to numerous stakeholders throughout the year, on a variety of issues, including, of course, legal disputes. But opinions often diverge between corporate lawyers and communicators on what constitutes good crisis management. The problems start with an often fundamentally different understanding of the legal assets to be protected and a lack of understanding of each other's professional approach.

(Slightly) exaggerated, the misunderstandings or divergent understandings of tasks between legal and communications departments are as follows.[8]

Potential disconnects between the communication department and legal department

Communication department	Legal department
Has to steer public debates in the interests of the company.	Publicity plays no role in the determination of legal positions in the first instance.
Feelings and emotion are important for the perception of the company. These are transported via "stories" and images.	Feelings are deliberately ignored, it is (only) a matter of deriving results in a legally clean manner.
Seeks to avoid the "Streisand effect": anyone who defends himself in court is only more likely to be in the public eye.	Claims are to be enforced in case of doubt.
Is under public expectation to explain himself quickly, it is about interpretative sovereignty to processes. Feels an impulse to act before public opinion has solidified. This results in pressure to talk to media representatives, for example. "He who is silent is wrong."	Fears deterioration of legal position due to rash statements. Time dimension is oriented to requirements of authorities and courts. "He who remains silent does not incriminate himself."
Reputation protection means also being able to admit mistakes.	Asset protection is in the foreground, reputation is not directly measurable and hence a "soft" asset.
Poorly able to assess legal risks due to lack of expertise.	Does not understand the dynamics of opinion formation.
Assumes that the legal department is indifferent to the company's reputation.	Assumes that everything the press department is told will be in the newspaper tomorrow and will damage the legal position.
Often has a cooperative relationship with journalists/external opinion leaders.	Sees itself in a defensive role vis-à-vis claimants.

At the heart of the matter is this question: How can the latent conflict between the protection of the asset position and the preservation of good reputation be reconciled? It is clear that corporate communications must keep an eye on the legal consequences of its actions, which already implies the need for close cooperation with the legal department – but to what extent is it the other way around?

Risk-minimizing factors in the cooperation between the legal and communications departments

There are a number of steps that can be taken in advance of a crisis to prepare and plan for the important collaboration between the legal and communications departments.

Establishment of a Reputation Risk Committee (RRC)

Many companies are attempting to rationally capture, assess, and prioritize the theoretically infinite array of reputational risks. Given the dynamic development in many industries and the constantly changing market environment, the political/regulatory framework and the fluid opinions of the relevant stakeholders, this is a very complex task. As an example, the energy industry is constantly facing new challenges in the area of tension between ecological requirements (climate change, European Green Deal), security of supply and profitability. A classic approach to managing reputation here is to internally assess how business decisions are likely to be perceived by shareholders, customers, the media, or society at large. Not to be forgotten, employees can also have their own unique perspective on a business decision, usually involving the impact on jobs and locations. A schematic list of reputation issues using the example of the energy industry illustrates how complex this can be.

Reputation topics for energy companies 2022: More risks than opportunities? Source: Brunswick

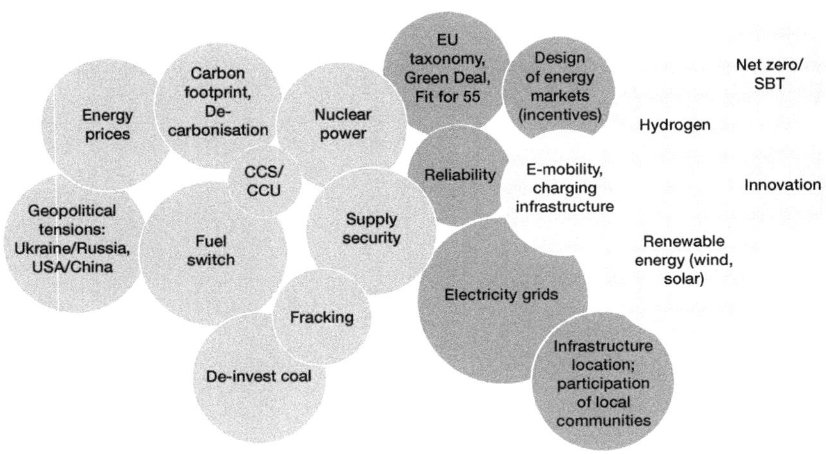

A Reputation Risk Committee is typically composed of representatives from the legal department, communications, the compliance department, and individual business divisions. It would establish its own rules of procedure, and announce the rules within the company that are important to its function. Importantly, the committee, via the help of the internal communications function, would appeal to all employees to bring business decisions with a potentially problematic reputational impact to the committee.

An important input for the ongoing work of the RRC are the reputation analyses available on the market, e.g., from RepRisk,[9] or the ESG ratings, e.g., from Sustainalytics[10] or MSCI.[11]

Clarification of responsibility for group companies

In staggered group companies, the problem is often that subsidiaries or even dependent branches do not want to be known in the context of problems at headquarters. This applies to operational failures, but even more so to reputational problems, which often also involve embarrassing human failures that are very likely to result in labor law action. It is humanly understandable to try to resolve the issue oneself as long as possible, or to hope that it will not become known. In contrast to this, however, is the danger to the reputation of the company as a whole. This is because the media tend to attribute the locally or decentrally occurring problem to the umbrella brand, the listed company as a whole, and thus to the group's management. Hence, the accusation of inadequate risk management and lack of supervision of the group as a whole quickly arises. To prevent an internal cover-up of reputational problems, almost all tiered group companies have drawn up internal rules on the level at which such issues must be resolved and who is to be informed or involved on the part of regional management or even the parent company. The figure overleaf illustrates such a process.

Best-practice crisis management process

Decision: do we have a crisis? →

Possible sources:
- Internal reporting line
- Media observation
- Reputation committee

Who manages the crisis internally? →

What is the impact of the issue?
- A local issue (fire in the building, issues with local contractor, HR-issue without connect to global values etc.)
  – Local crisis team responsible
- A regional issue (all subsidiaries in the region affected, e.g., Cyber attack)
  – Regional crisis team responsible
- A global issue (problem originates in one location, but triggers questions of global risk management and oversight (accounting standards, Code of Business Conduct etc.))
  – Global crisis team responsible

Useful criteria: will stakeholders in other locations be interested in the story?

↓

What is the potential threat?
- How could the situation effect:
  - Stakeholder's confidence?
  - The company's financial position of cashflow?
  - Management's ability to run the company?
- What response could it provoke from journalists and/or stakeholders on social media?

↓

Convene crisis team
Include those required to bring situation under control and communicate with key audiences

↓

Short term activities
- Who are the stakeholders?
- Express sympathy with disadvantaged persons/ victims
- Investigate facts
- Prepare written statements in line with developing truth about the issue

Ongoing crisis management
As solution develops, communicate about:
- Your findings as they evolve
- Actions being taken
- Resolution to be expected

Crisis manual

Crisis manuals, especially in large corporations, clearly prescribe in advance the rules according to which crisis management, including communication, is to be carried out; this has an effect on both the legal and communications departments. Such a crisis manual usually has the following subsections.

Recommended elements of a crisis manual

Version control	Who is the author? Date of the respective applicable rule, documentation of any adjustments made.
Description of objectives	Explanation of the importance of reputation protection, definition of responsibilities, reference to compliance with globally or regionally applicable rules.
Scope	To which units does the crisis manual apply? (usually directly to all units operating under the global brand, sub-brands might follow different rules).
Definitions	Reputation, risks, but also image opportunities.
Standards for reputation management	Examples: • Principle that each local unit is responsible for managing its own reputation issues (otherwise damaging separation of causation and repair). • Focus on particularly sensitive issues defined in advance for the Group. • Obligation to observe issue papers on, for example, critical ESG issues, compliance, HR rules, etc. (to avoid deviating messages). • Duty to follow "best practice", e.g., constant monitoring of digital platforms such as Twitter, LinkedIn, etc. • Duty to report reputational opportunities in the respective local market.
Recommendation on the establishment of crisis teams	• What is a crisis team? In which units should it be set up? • Description of best-practices for organizing crisis teams.
Contacts	List of names, addresses, telephone numbers, email addresses of those responsible for crisis management in the event of an emergency (both office and private contacts).

Cooperation between the legal and communications departments in the event of a crisis

Once a crisis has been reported and identified, the protection of reputation depends critically on the speed of coordinated response. The more one can rely on pre-established plans and procedures, the more energy one can devote to the numerous activities that must be carried out spontaneously. On the other hand, the application of a crisis plan must also not be too mechanistic; under no circumstances should a situation arise in which a previously prepared plan obscures the view of the differences in the concrete situation now at hand and prefabricated lists are simply "checked off".

Professional crisis management typically involves the following steps.

Determination: Do we have a crisis?

Even the decision as to whether a crisis exists at all is difficult to make in individual cases. It is advisable at this point to consult the various positions in the company (communications department, legal department, marketing managers, sales department (as the "voice of the customer"), IT, HR department, etc.). Under no circumstances should one be guided by the often encountered motivation to seek blame from others, to enter into a kind of denial posture, to not describe oneself as affected. Exemplary in this context was the reaction of Germanwings after the accident in 2015, with which the company accepted responsibility immediately after the crash, although the cause was still completely unclear. One danger here lies in so-called "compartmentalization" in which the corporate headquarters attempts to shift responsibility to a division or subsidiary and does not claim to be affected or responsible (the *Exxon Valdez* case, 1989). Criteria for a crisis determination may include the severity of the incident, the degree of possible misconduct, and the initial response of relevant stakeholders.

Convening the crisis team

Once a crisis has been identified, it is important to get all members of the crisis team around the table very quickly. It is advisable to practice this once or twice a year beforehand. A room reserved for this purpose with appropriate technical equipment should be provided. The crisis team leader is responsible for coordination. It is important for both the legal department and the communications department to determine in advance who from the two areas is to be involved in supporting the crisis team. Just as different employees are responsible for special topics in the legal department, there are also regularly very differentiated responsibilities in the communications department (strategic planning, media relations, internal communications, social media, central responsibility for content, to name just the most important).

Media monitoring

The first measure on the part of the communications department is to monitor and evaluate the relevant media, including social media, and to send them to the crisis team at regular intervals. The question of whether and how the crisis topic is being discussed in the media, and which protagonists/antagonists are positioning themselves is an essential input for calibrating one's own response.

Creation of communication materials

Experience shows that the beginning of a crisis situation is characterized by great uncertainty. Usually it is not known at all, or only in outline, what actually happened, and who is responsible for what. Nevertheless, it is important to start preparing communication documents immediately, even if it is clear to everyone that these are still subject to change. It is also important to come up with as comprehensive a list of critical questions as possible, even if they are uncomfortable or touch on critical issues ("Did the CEO know about this? Why didn't he know about this?"). Not wanting to ask yourself these questions, or not daring to ask them, does not mean journalists or regulators won't ask them. Repression of unpleasant truths is the worst thing that can happen at this stage, because it leads to passive, disingenuous communication down the road.

Parallel to the creation of the narrative and the question/answer catalog, there is an examination of one's own legal position, even if this can only be done in a cursory manner given the short time available. Do claims exist against the company? Conversely, does the company have claims against others?

Ongoing decision – communication or silence?

This is regularly the most difficult question, especially since in most cases the company's own interest is to prevent discussion of the problem and the visibility of its own brand in the media as far as possible. However, it is also clear that, at a certain point, one's own silence is understood as an admission of guilt, arrogance, or a sign of lack of empathy for the victims (if they exist). Criteria for the question of whether one must speak out are:[12]

- Are there legal obligations (e.g., GDPR? Duties to inform capital markets?).
- Do those close to us (customers, shareholders, employees) expect us to say something?
- Are others already talking about us? Is an opinion being formed? (Is there a threat of losing the authority to interpret?).
- Is silence interpreted as a sign of guilt?

When it comes to the question, "React or remain silent?" it is of great importance whether only one's own company is affected (e.g., via a compliance violation) or the entire industry has a problem (e.g., due to new regulation). The "golden rule" of crisis communication requires the greatest possible transparency and proactivity in the event of a crisis. Because only then do journalists and other observers recognize that the company itself has an interest in clarification (rather than wanting to "cover up" the circumstances). However, if the entire industry is affected, the situation is different. In that case, you don't want to be the first to publicize the problem (then the topic is perceived as "the {Brand Name} problem"), nor do you want to be the last to be accused of wanting to distance yourself from the topic, unlike everyone else. Compare it with a school of fish when the shark comes along – he will bite the individual fish that are outside the swirling and confusing large main body of the school. Also important can be the question of whether the crisis-triggering circumstance arose within or outside the company. The more own responsibility exists, the more stakeholders expect proactive, problem- and solution-oriented communication.

It is helpful that either the managers or the crisis officers from the legal and communications departments are in regular contact in order to identify crisis starting points in good time. These can be new products (risk of recall), customer complaints, shareholder lawsuits, media inquiries, the expected voting behavior of voting agencies, and a virtually infinite number of other sources of a reputational crisis. In the event of a crisis, it is important not to create a race for internal attention. Central departments such as legal, communications, and HR, for example, are often in unspoken competition for the board's favor. The last thing that is needed in the event of a crisis is disgruntlement among each other, because the respective other positions itself past the crisis team with the executive board, provides for uncoordinated preliminary determinations, and uses the crisis for profiling at the expense of its colleagues from the neighboring department.

What is the most effective way to protect one's reputation?

In the past, government agencies were expected to be rule-oriented, and companies were expected to be efficient. Today, both are required to do both – the state must also act efficiently, and companies are required to comply with social norms, to which the pursuit of profit must be subordinated. When a company is in crisis, it is often too late. The decisive factor is whether it has presented itself sufficiently to the public in the years before, made clear what it does, why it is important, and according to which ethical rules it acts. A company that pursues the "submerged whale strategy" ("If you are not visible, you cannot be harpooned") in the years leading up to a crisis has not understood the mechanics of public opinion. We live in times of hyper-transparency, in which, unlike in the past, any misconduct is very likely to become visible and known – a welcome development – be it through "whistleblowers", higher control density, reporting obligations, compliance training, etc. Critical comments, at least on social media, are unavoidable, and from there they regularly find their way into journalism. Every company must be particularly aware of the importance of opinion-leading media. These are quality media such as the *Financial Times*, *The Economist*, *The Wall Street Journal*, the *Frankfurter Allgemeine Zeitung*, and many others. It is good risk management to be present in these media constantly and with as many different topics and people as possible, so that when a crisis is picked up by such media with high relevance and reach, the named company is not exclusively associated with this problem in the perception of the target groups. The impact of the bad news is rather being diluted, as it will be put in context of a long series of contrasting positive articles on the company's purpose, strategy, values, management personnel, etc.

This is not the task of the legal department, but it should support it to the best of its ability.

References

1 Nikolaus von Bomhard, Schwarzer Schwan und Vogel Strauss ("Black Swan and Ostrich"), *Frankfurter Allgemeine Zeitung*, 1 April 2016, Christian Lawrence, Nach der Krise ist vor der Krise ("After the crisis is before the crisis"), *Frankfurter Allgemeine Zeitung*, 8 April 2020.

2 Volker Boehme-Nessler, Litigation und Kommunikation: Zusammenarbeit von Kommunikations- und Rechtsabteilungen in Unternehmen, in Zerfaß/Piwinger, *Handbuch Unternehmenskommunikation*, Springer 2014, S.1321.

3 Martin Wohlrabe, Litigation PR, 2020.

4 Random examples: Barclays, EnBW, SAP, Allianz, see Ernst/Fischer/Baumgartner, FAZ.Net 3.3.2021.

5 www.agcs.allianz.com/news-and-insights/reports/allianz-risk-barometer.html

6 Helio Fred Garcia, *The Power of Communication*, 2012, p.72.

7 Emilio Galli-Zugaro, *The Listening Leader*, 2017, p.4.

8 Table adapted from Boehme-Nessler, Footnote 2, p.1,328.

9 www.reprisk.com

10 www.sustainalytics.com

11 www.msci.com

12 Helio Fred Garcia, *The Power of Communication*, 2012, p.100.

Chapter 9:

Workforce management of the future – virtual teams, hybrid working, and the future workforce

By Robert Loef, group general counsel, Best Secret Group AG, and Anne Meckbach, chief compliance officer, ProSiebenSat.1 Group

COVID-19 as change agent

Aside from the terrible and gruesome toll of COVID-19 on mankind's health and wellbeing, the pandemic provided for an unprecedented impromptu social experiment, changing the working environment of the service industry and administrative functions across all industries almost worldwide. People who regularly saw and interacted with each other in person on an everyday basis, had to start – sometimes literally overnight – to replace that personal with virtual interaction. Luckily, almost all technology necessary to address that tectonic shift in workplace reality was readily available and even in use for specific use cases such as long-distance meetings or negotiations. The great innovation, however, forcefully brought forward by the pandemic, is the sudden ubiquity of virtual communication within teams that until then had been defined by personal interactions.

"It's not personal, it's strictly business"

The power of the Godfather's youngest son's most famous quote derives from the fact that it turns the traditionally held belief "All business is personal" on its head. When it comes to pre-pandemic corporate work ethics, there were few exceptions to the rule that physical presence is a cornerstone of building successful teams and organizations. This was particularly true for the legal profession, and even more so for in-house legal functions, as the nature and content of legal workstreams are generally highly confidential and of tangible impact to the whole organization, respectively. Consequently, a pre-pandemic (rare) day of remote work was more of a theoretical option or sometimes even a euphemistic description for "a day off". Social distancing then taught us quickly that if you strip the in-house function to its bare bones, its tasks generally do not require a high degree of onsite presence but rather little more than a computer and a stable internet connection. As a result, the overwhelming majority of in-house legal counsel in both the US and Europe has been working from home for the last two years.

(Preliminary) tenets for future workforce management

The outcome of this social experiment is still very much in flux, as a world you can securely call post-pandemic is unfortunately still utopian. However, when structuring the new "normal" and building legal teams in the future, the following tenets may serve as guiding principles:

- Teams can work together productively and cohesively without being in the office, day-in, day-out.
- Hybrid work poses specific challenges to the legal department, which can be overcome by the right policies and technology.
- (Predominantly) remote work has a corrosive effect on loyalty and sense of belonging.
- Leadership needs to empower, not control, people.
- Business unit embedded teams are more important than ever to avoid being siloed.
- Different jobs/tasks require different workplace models.

In the following, we will detail why we consider these tenets to be meaningful for every general counsel staffing and managing its team.

Before diving into the details, however, we would like to clarify the terminology we use going forward and note a clear distinction – we will use "remote work" for work that is exclusively being done away from the office and "hybrid work" for any kind of mix of work being performed in the office and away from the office. Similarly, we will use the term "remote teams" for teams who only collaborate virtually and "hybrid teams" who work together in a mix of virtual and personal interaction.

Teams can work together productively and cohesively without being in the office, day-in, day-out

One fallacy in the beginning of the pandemic, particularly in bigger enterprises with large legal departments, was for the general counsel to assume that the way she/he managed geographically disparate teams remotely could simply be mirrored for managing the teams (and management within those teams) in headquarters. Even in pre-pandemic times, general counsel of multinational conglomerates had to cope with managing remote teams as they had national or regional legal leads (and their teams) reporting to them who they barely got to see in-person. In most cases, the regular collaboration between the general counsel with remote offices is limited to a few reporting calls a month and the actual workstreams in those offices are separable from headquarters.

This, however, is not a system that can be copied/pasted into a team that thrived on personal interaction. The workstreams at headquarters are generally deeply intertwined with the other administrative or business units and there are a lot of ties and exchanges between team members that fall away when there is no personal interaction.

To state the obvious – despite the above, the lack of preparation and the social and mental distress of the pandemic, the shift to remote working in the legal departments still worked and was almost spectacularly unspectacular. Across the board, there was little to no disruption in the maintenance of legal services in-house. So, the first important take-away is, working remotely both individually and as a team, even on a 100 percent basis and for an extended period of time, is possible.

A question that is more difficult to answer, though, is if working remotely works better, i.e., more effectively/efficiently etc. than working at the office. Here it seems like the manifold upsides of remote working (increased flexibility, avoiding a commute, bigger hiring universe, more diverse teams etc.) are met with as many downsides (less accountability/control, less identification with employer/team etc.).

While remote work caused by long distance will remain as a matter of necessity, remote work due to COVID-19 fell away, bringing about the necessity for general counsel to decide if they provide rules and guardrails or just let the workforce make their own decisions or follow the decisions on a company-wide level. We think it does make sense, while respecting the personal freedom and sense of responsibility of the workforce, to introduce certain rules and guardrails as we consider them important to fostering a positive and sustainable working environment. This is why, in the following, we argue (little surprisingly) that neither the "old way" of working at the office 100 percent nor full remote working is the optimal choice, but rather a clearly defined hybrid working policy, combining a large degree of freedom of the legal team or team member to organize its work while encouraging personal interaction and making a minimum of such interaction mandatory.

In this context it is worth noting that the legal department will in most instances not be in a position to determine singlehandedly (if at all) which organizational model to follow, but instead will have to integrate its own processes into the company's general policies (or simply follow the latter).

Such policies will in many cases not only allow for "the one" perfect solution. In these cases, it will be necessary (and possible) for the general counsel to weigh its options in order to create a work environment that is perceived to be positive and enabling by the employees.

Another reason for a hybrid work model is the "war for talent" that also rages in the legal profession. Legal departments face fierce competition from other legal professions, in particular law firms, which on average offer higher salaries. Therefore, recruitment of highly qualified and motivated (future) employees and their retention is a challenge. Employees will be looking in detail at the other upsides that an in-house job may offer. One of these upsides could very well be a (more) flexible work environment, which allows for hybrid work and therefore, for example, reduces the requirement to commute and integrates more easily with family life.

Hybrid work poses specific challenges to the legal department, which can be overcome by the right policies and technology

The balancing of remote and hybrid working models with traditional office-based work and the integration of such models in the processes of a legal department is likely to impose additional challenges – from an organizational, procedural, and legal perspective. The legal challenges associated with remote and hybrid work are manifold and will vary in detail from jurisdiction to jurisdiction, while the respective legal frameworks are currently extremely dynamic due to ongoing political discussions. Any attempt to provide a comprehensive list or even assessment here would therefore be bound to fail. The related challenges may include questions related to various different issues, such as:

- *Labor law.* May I ask my employee to work remotely or onsite? Are labor unions or works councils potentially to be involved in the process?
- *Data security.* Do I need consent from employees participating in hybrid meetings with regard to the use of cameras?
- *Workplace security.* Inspections of remote workplaces may be next to impossible.
- *Tax law.* Is the level of taxation of the company dependent on the place from which the employees perform their assignments and could this potentially even have an impact on the company's COMI?
- *Insurance law.* Does insurance cover workplace accidents outside the company's premises?

Such challenges will be intensified if employees not only request to not work onsite but instead from their home, a co-working or public space, but from abroad, i.e., from another country/jurisdiction for days, weeks, or even months. When setting up any new working model, the legal department will therefore likely be involved – be it as a user of such new model or as one of the departments assessing the possibility and implications of any chosen model.

(Predominantly) remote work has a corrosive effect on loyalty and sense of belonging

On the other hand, purely remote work obviously also has downsides, in particular for those employees who are less outspoken and therefore tend to reach out less to colleagues or superiors as well as for junior colleagues who will not have the opportunity to "watch and learn" in the same way as this would be true would they be sharing an office with more senior colleagues. Downsides for the general counsel are, besides the fact that she/he may also suffer from a lack of teamwork and interaction, a lower degree of feedback from and control over his or her workforce. Without presence in the office, the opportunity for certain members of the group to do less than their "fair share" is certainly bigger than in a highly (socially) controlled office environment. This is especially true in departments in which employees are not all based at headquarters and where some employees are maybe asked more frequently to work onsite than others.

Only looking at these advantages and disadvantages (and knowing that there will be more of each category) of remote work vs onsite work, it will be the task of each general counsel to find the "right" balance between remote and onsite work, i.e., to create a hybrid work environment that will be perceived by the majority of employees as generally beneficial.

A particular challenge is to foster team spirit in an environment where colleagues only meet seldomly or maybe never. Such groups lack common experiences and are likely to not truly perceive each other as a team. While this may be a less pleasant work environment, it has (at least) two obvious disadvantages to be considered:

- Employees of any department which do not have any team experience are more likely to change positions quickly. What may seem like an advantage in the war for talent, i.e., the opportunity to work remotely, may backfire with regard to retention.
- There will be less casual conversation between team members.

Besides the fact that this is important with regard to the fostering of team experiences, it should not be underestimated how much relevant information regarding ongoing work issues is conveyed during such interaction or due to the fact that team members share an office. If teams are not interacting enough, the very real risk exists that the relevant information does not flow and (legal) risks materialize due to a lack of information sharing.

However, it is not easy to foster team spirit in a virtual environment without the efforts being too artificial. One solution would be to have more or less regular real-life meetings, such as a regular team day; the other alternative is to create opportunities for virtual interactions. Very likely, a "one size fits all" solution will not be possible and individual solutions will need to be found, without sacrificing the team spirit altogether. Another component to team spirit is work on joint assignments by certain team members, potentially alternating teams in order for in particular junior members to get to know other team members and to get an overview of the variety of tasks within the department. In particular, junior members are likely to profit from such interaction.

Leadership needs to empower, not control, people

Maybe most importantly, general counsel will have to adapt their leadership culture to the new reality of not being able to micromanage their teams and processes. While this lesson should have been learned long ago, in a hybrid working environment any other leadership approach is a losing proposition to begin with. Hybrid teams will thrive if they can act as a unit without having to wait for directions from the top. General counsel have to let go and create relationships built on trust and not authority to manage the workflows effectively and efficiently.

Teams also profit a lot from being freed from middle management. Instead of having multiple levels of reporting lines, teams need to be able to self-organize according to the respective tasks they are working on. This is enabled by modern matrix organizations in which legal functions not only report within the legal department but are also closely embedded in one or more business units depending on their expertise/tasks. Particularly, legal counsel who as a rule have a deep understanding of their respective area of expertise should be able to accomplish their tasks without a lot of supervision. In building teams, even more than before, general counsel need to strike a good balance of seniority within teams to enable a transfer of know-how and experience.

One other key element of this leadership culture is sharing information early and communicating a lot. Teams need to have the full picture in order to get their job done. Of course, not all information can be shared at any time with anybody but while, traditionally, general counsel erred on the side of caution, it is time to err on the side of empowerment by sharing the necessary information at the right time, albeit always within the boundaries of applicable statutory law, such as insider rules and regulations.

Another tradition that significantly hinders hybrid collaboration is "over"-reporting. While the top-down flow of information is traditionally a challenge, as laid out above, the bottom-up flow of information, aka reporting, is often over-emphasized. While it is understandable and essential for the general counsel to be informed on all relevant topics within its department, the time it takes to filter up such information is usually blown out of proportion. One way to tackle this issue is to use tools common in other (tech) departments which are used by teams to self-organize to simultaneously serve as reporting tools, such as Kanban boards. Used effectively, this also provides the general counsel to have real time KPIs on the service levels of its entire team to the extent possible under applicable labor law.

Business unit embedded teams are more important than ever to avoid being siloed

Similarly, a key driver for effectively working in hybrid teams is that they are not only hybrid in terms of where the team members work but also hybrid in how they are staffed with legal and non-legal professionals. This applies not only within the legal department in which it is necessary to diversify teams according to their tasks, e.g., staff the corporate legal department not only with legal counsel, but also have specialized portfolio managers and paralegals as well as a corporate secretary function. In other areas of the legal department, it even means forging teams out of legal counsel and operational functions, such as direct or indirect procurement or distribution. The more embedded the legal teams are, the better they understand how they can add value and drive the business.

This way of working is particularly encouraged in companies that are structured as a matrix organization. In such organizations, employees work in cross-functional teams and thus have multiple reporting lines (one solid and one or more dotted lines). In the legal department, this means that legal counsel, while remaining independent in rendering legal advice, are embedded in the teams that they provide legal advice to.

Different jobs/tasks need different workplace models

Obviously, it would be a possibility to stick, respectively return, to the "old normal", asking employees of the legal department to work onsite five days a week, respectively, in larger groups that do not only have offices at one location, to schedule regular in-person meetings requiring travel, e.g., once per week to head office. However, such a culture would most likely be regarded as a downside by (future) employees, who have first-hand experience that it is not necessary to follow this model to have a well-functioning legal department. To the extent the company's general policies allow for hybrid working models, shaping a work environment that positively encompasses both worlds will be a challenge.

The list of further possible or perceived advantages of hybrid work is long and reaches from the more general "better work–life balance", less distractions from general "background noise" in the office, the hope to be able to recruit more women for jobs which they may have turned down in the past fearing that they may not be able to satisfy both the demands of the job and their family, over the potentially reduced need of companies to provide office space for 100 percent of its staff, to more macroeconomic considerations such as that the pressure on highly competitive housing markets in larger cities may be lifted if rural sites become more attractive for employees due to a minimal requirement to commute, which again may reduce the need to pay extraordinary high wages, up to environmental considerations (less emissions due to less travel). Last, not least, for larger organizations, hybrid teams offer the possibility for individual members to specialize in certain fields. While any type of specific expertise may not be needed frequently enough at one location to allow for such specialization, it may be required across the organization and the possibility to deploy such abilities also remotely for other group companies or sub-departments may justify a specialized role, whereas as otherwise the respective special advice would have to be retained externally in each case.

The relevance of the office and the possibility to work onsite is likely to shift in the future from the everyday workplace to a place of active professional and social interaction. This will also mean that the infrastructure onsite may have to be adapted to cater to these changed needs. While the single or double office was long regarded as the gold standard, this is likely not to be true going forward – not least due to the changed role of onsite work. A work environment that actively promotes exchange, interaction, and networking will be more relevant, while (and if) employees are able to perform their assignments for which they need a quieter environment may do so remotely. If the relevant team leads are able to create such an environment, onsite work may be regarded as a positive diversion instead of a chore.

The general counsel will have to make sure that remote work is not seized by certain team members as a welcome opportunity to shift their workload to others or to generally underperform due to a lack of supervision. While this is less likely to happen in an environment in which employees perceive themselves as team members (see above), simple methods like regular check-ins and briefings can be used to make sure that the workload is attributed evenly. Also, such meetings may serve as an institutionalized forum for team members to exchange information and update each other on relevant developments. Often, this will lead to the opportunity to work on assignments jointly. The smaller the teams are and the more similar the topics are on which the individual members work, the more frequent should these meetings be. In larger groups or with very diverse fields of expertise, less meetings will be better to avoid meeting fatigue. Certain IT tools or techniques borrowed from the agile work environment may be beneficial to structure such information sharing. Besides that, each team lead will need to make sure to reserve sufficient time in his or her calendar for non-purely business-related issues of team members also in a remote or hybrid work environment. For such purposes, it may be a solution to reserve certain time slots each week for the team members and encourage them to "drop in" should they wish to discuss anything with their superior.

As most solutions for legal departments are likely to encompass some sort of hybrid work, it will be necessary to provide the needed infrastructure (i.e., meeting rooms equipped with suitable cameras) and to stipulate clear rules for hybrid meetings (e.g., regarding the use of cameras or timings). While some of these measures are likely to be part of a general company policy – as may be the provision of the required equipment – the general counsel should proactively stipulate the necessary rules and procedures reflecting the individual circumstances of the legal department.

In summary, the technological solutions allow to leverage the advantages of remote and onsite work with the aim of creating a more beneficial work environment, resulting in better work results, satisfied employees, and thus higher retention without sacrificing team spirit and risking the steady flow of information.

Even drastically disruptive events tend to trigger evolutionary change rather than revolutionary change. Translated into the evolving ways of working for businesses as a whole, and legal departments in particular, this leads to an increased acceptance of hybrid work. Still, there will be a continued need and desire of both staff and management to foster personal interaction. So, on balance, while Michael Corleone certainly has a point when differentiating between personal and business relationships, managing hybrid teams involves both. Physical presence provides a social glue that is not easily eradicated from our reptilian brain.

Chapter 10:
ESG – how the GC and legal function contribute to sustainability initiatives

By E. Leigh Dance, founder and executive director, Global Counsel Leaders

In January 2020, the Global Counsel Leaders' bi-annual benchmark[1] of corporate legal chiefs in larger companies and institutions in 12 countries revealed its expectation that ESG would be one of three top issues consuming their time in the year ahead.

I was stunned by this response to a write-in question. The top three issues presented pre-pandemic (with the first two being no surprise) were:

1. Cybersecurity;
2. Complex regulations; and
3. Various words describing "environmental and social issues, and sustainability-related governance".

The year 2020 saw a dramatic rise in ESG-focused investing, a focus on employee wellbeing, and an emphasis on stakeholder priorities versus shareholder priorities. By the end of 2020, the *Financial Times* had added "Climate" to its front-page menu options, between "Markets" and "Opinion".

The investment sector has led the ESG movement at the same time as the public has increasingly raised concerns on climate change and key social issues of the day. Regulators have been catching up quickly, including now in the US.

To guide general counsel navigating the fast and winding ESG speedway, this chapter has four parts:

1. Why ESG requires your attention.
2. Key elements of ESG – the main elements, drawn from my organization's three years of research and reporting on ESG for general counsel, their teams, and legal service providers.

3. The general counsel's evolving role in ESG – how general counsel are contributing to their organizations' ESG activities.
4. Setting priorities and structure for ESG in legal – tips and guidance to help general counsel design a structure, narrow focus, and take action where most needed.

Part 1: Why ESG requires your attention

For the general counsel that questions ESG as a business trend and their need to participate in ESG in some way, the points below are meant to change their views.

Global ESG assets may surpass $41 trillion by 2022 and $50 trillion by 2025, one-third of the projected total assets under management globally, according to a new report by Bloomberg Intelligence.[2] Investing in companies with higher ESG ratings is correlated with higher financial returns. The Morgan Stanley Capital International (MSCI) World ESG Leaders' Index, for example, rose by 22 percent as of late 2021, compared with the MSCI World Index's (not ESG) gain of 15 percent over the same period.[3]

A Stanford University study of 70 general counsel (diverse industries, 75 percent with revenues over $US1bn) found that 72 percent somewhat or strongly believe ESG efforts will improve their companies' long-term financial performance. The study reported that 63 percent of CEOs in respondent organizations have taken a vocal, public stance on environmental (43 percent), societal (29 percent), or political (7 percent) issues unrelated to the company's core business.[4]

Bloomberg Intelligence reported that assets invested in ESG might surpass $41 trillion in 2022.[5] Much of that money is held in Europe, the Middle East, and Africa, reflecting the region's earlier adoption of the ESG investing trend as well as regulation far more advanced than the US. The US is catching up fast.

Confusion about ESG investments

While many today are questioning various issues in the wide world of ESG and particularly the investment sector, many of these issues will be resolved over time. It is likely that the true positive sustainability impact will come with regulation, where double materiality[6] plays a fundamental part.

The primary misunderstanding is that nearly all investment products labelled with ESG (thus higher fees) focus solely on how ESG is projected to impact the company's or institution's performance. Examples are climate-change related disasters, supply chain disruption due to climate change, or negative impacts of social issues such as discrimination or human slavery. ESG fund focus currently only very rarely includes the company's own actions to reduce negative impact on the environment, social, or related governance.[7]

Many factors drive growing importance of ESG

A 2021 study by PWC and London Business School found that half of the FTSE 100 link executive pay to progress on E, S and G targets.[8] Stakeholders and shareholders are demanding proof of progress.[9] In 2021, Governance and Accountability Institute's research found that 92 percent of the Fortune 500 produced and distributed a Sustainability Report, as did 70 percent of the Russell Global 100®.[10] Those reports become more sophisticated every day (as do the regulatory agencies and investment analysts that read them).

Boston Consulting Group research finds that consumers and investors across all ages, not just Generation Z, seek products and services from sellers with strong sustainability scores – from finance to food to fashion.[11] BCG research concludes that 38 percent of consumers have already changed to clothing brands whose ESG practices they rate higher.[12] An early 2020 study by First Insight revealed that most millennials and Gen Z (62 percent) prefer to buy from sustainable brands.[13]

To sum up: the general counsel that treats ESG solely as compliance, altruism, or corporate responsibility (philanthropy) not only takes an enormous risk, but misses the opportunity to be a valued advocate for her company.

Sustainability moves to harder-edge policy, regulatory, and litigative era

Paul Clements-Hunt, CEO of The Blended Capital Group and one of two (with Professor Paul Watchman) at the UN who coined the ESG term back in 2004, describes this dynamic:

> *"The essential point is that the legal system around sustainability has moved from the market-facing, nudge it forward, voluntary initiatives of the past three decades – along with grand multilateral statements and aspirations – into a much harder-edged policy, regulatory and litigative era."*[14]

So, what next? It's futile for your legal team to try to stay up to date on the massive, messy, and constantly-changing ESG movement and its regulation. It is likely to be at least three years before the clouds clear and the noise becomes reasonable. Much of that clarity will come from regulation. Meanwhile, you must choose how to prioritize key areas that affect your core business and matter to your stakeholders – then be ready to revise the priorities as events occur.

We have seen general counsel successfully weather many major changes in global regulation in the 21st century already – Sarbanes Oxley in the US, anti-corruption and data privacy regulation globally are just a few examples. *You can do this!*

Part 2: Key elements of ESG for general counsel

> *"ESG is an acronym for Environmental, Social, and Governance. ESG takes the holistic view that sustainability extends beyond just environmental issues."*[15]

It initially was a structure to refer to three key factors to measure the sustainability and ethical impact of an investment in a business or company. From the coining of the ESG term in 2004 by Paul Clements-Hunt and Paul Watchman at the United Nations Environment Program Finance Initiative (UNEP FI), the concept has emphasized the complex connection between the three factors, particularly in terms of impact on risk and opportunity.

A new way of looking at capitalism

ESG presents a new way of looking at capitalism, by giving as much attention to stakeholder needs (customers, employees, regulatory agencies, etc.) as it does to shareholders. Developing ESG regulation often views ESG criteria alongside the typical concept of fiduciary duty. Traditional financial reporting is increasingly merging with what are sometimes called "non-financial factors" (such as the E, S, and G), given the conclusion that these non-traditional factors eventually hit the organization's bottom line.

Regulators who request reporting on the company's ESG performance increasingly seek data from the enterprise from two distinct sides of risk, called "double materiality". These two sides are:

1. How the company will impact both the environment and society (with the expectation that, year-to-year, the company will show that it is **doing less harm** to both); and
2. How ESG factors will create risks that could have an impact on the company's financial performance.

Scenarios for the effect of these risks on a company's business model and operations are:

- #1 Risk: The impact that the company's business or farming or fossil fuel extraction activities pose to the environment and society. For example, improper disposal of hazardous chemicals that damage local water supplies.
- #2 Risk: The company's facilities are located on coastlines in hurricane risk zones that will face far higher insurance premiums and potential production outages during storms.

Financial materiality

The EU's new Corporate Sustainability Reporting Directive regulation, due to go live in 2023, will require comprehensive ESG disclosures by nearly 50,000 European companies (and all companies listed in the EU) that include disclosing double materiality.

In early 2022, Carmen Nuzzo, head of fixed income investment practices at Principles for Responsible Investing (PRI, an organization with over 4,500 signatories representing $120 trillion of assets under management), describes the additional concept of financial materiality:

> *"Investors and other stakeholders increasingly accept that ESG factors can be financially material because they present significant risks for companies, either through direct financial/legal liabilities or through negative reputational effects."*[16]

ESG factors are a subset of non-financial performance (Nuzzo calls them non-traditional performance indicators) that include ethical, sustainable, and corporate government issues such as making sure there are systems in place to ensure accountability and managing the corporation's carbon footprint.

Many readers may know already the ESG definitions, so skip forward. The below is combined from a half-dozen reliable websites:

Environmental criteria examine how a business performs as a steward of our natural environment, focusing on:

- Waste and pollution;
- Resource stewardship of energy, water, forestation, animal habitats, etc.;

- Greenhouse gas emission (direct and indirect, e.g., through the supply chain);
- Use of toxins in products; and
- Resilience against physical climate change risks (e.g., fires, floods, hurricanes).

Social criteria consider societal and stakeholders' interests in how the company treats key ethical and employee issues, and customer interests, regarding:

- Employee wellbeing;
- Diversity, equity, and inclusion;
- Working conditions, including child labor and slavery;
- Local communities; funding or support of projects or institutions helping poor and underserved communities globally; and
- Health and safety.

Governance criteria examine how a corporation is led and managed, so that board and executive decision-making processes, internal controls and processes all promote transparency and accountability. Governance increasingly includes how leadership's incentives are aligned to stakeholder expectations. Topics covered may include:

- Tax strategy;
- Executive remuneration;
- Donations and political lobbying;
- Scrutiny of CEO and executive stance on environmental, social and political issues;
- Controls on bribery and other forms of corruption; and
- Board diversity and structure.

ESG is essentially a framework that helps people and organizations see how an organization is managing risks and opportunities related to environmental, social, and governance criteria. Stakeholders include customers, suppliers, regulators, and employees as well as the investment community.

Growing consideration of link between profit and purpose

Lex Mundi's excellent analysis of this trend is summed up here:

> *"Continued societal focus on issues of sustainability is leading to the rewriting of the rules of global capitalism and the emergence of a new economic paradigm. These trends indicate that boards and leadership teams may increasingly come to rely upon general counsel to serve as a bridge to diverse stakeholder communities in order to support market positions, deal with ambitious supply chain compliance, and foster a culture that is conducive to sustainability imperatives."*[17]

Black Rock CEO, Larry Fink, wrote at the start of 2022:

> *"Stakeholder capitalism is not about politics. It is not a social or ideological agenda. It is not "woke". It is capitalism, driven by mutually beneficial relationships between you and the employees, customers, suppliers, and communities your company relies on to prosper. This is the power of capitalism."*

Fink continues:

> *"We focus on sustainability not because we're environmentalists, but because we are capitalists and fiduciaries to our clients. That requires understanding how companies are adjusting their businesses for the massive changes the economy is undergoing. As part of that focus, we are asking companies to set short-, medium-, and long-term targets for greenhouse gas reductions. These targets, and the quality of plans to meet them, are critical to the long-term economic interests of your shareholders."*[18]

Black Rock also announced in this letter that it expects organizations it invests in to report consistently with the Task Force on Climate-Related Financial Disclosures (TCFD) rules.

Defining stakeholder capitalism, an element of the ESG concept

General counsel should take note of the trend by companies towards acceptance that ESG issues are business performance issues. Underscoring that is the growing recognition of how profit and purpose are interconnected – or what Lex Mundi calls Enterprise Values vs Enterprise Value.[19]

Countless research studies over the last few years demonstrate that investing in companies with higher ESG ratings is correlated with higher financial returns (a causal relationship, however, is still unproven).

ESG as converging systemic risks

According to Paul Clements-Hunt, the world is at a fundamental juncture, as ongoing waves of COVID-19 reveal our civilization's fragility and its inequality. "*Long-term sovereign, investment sector, and citizen assets are being challenged and undermined like never before by converging systemic risks*," says Clements-Hunt.

Clements-Hunt finds that policy makers have concluded that sustainable business must center around our response to these risks. They are now taking climate change, ecosystems destruction, resource depletion, and a whole plethora of interconnected social challenges much more seriously.

"*Think ESG not in E-S-G silos*," says Clements-Hunt. He recommends that in-house counsel can best use ESG as a powerful lens to bring both converging risks and associated new economy opportunities into high resolution for your organizations.

He adds:

> "*For example, climate is as much a wicked social problem as it is environmental and needs robust corporate governance if global supply chain risks are to be well managed. How so? Take mining: climate is impacting now the vulnerable communities in Africa who will dig up the strategic minerals to decarbonize the G20 economies.*"[20]

A 2021 meta-analysis of 1,000+ studies co-performed by NYU Stern's Center and shared in their Sustainable Business' ESG and Financial Performance report[21] has several findings of significance for corporate legal and compliance leaders, including:

- ESG investing provides downside protection, especially during a social or economic crisis;
- ESG disclosures alone, without an accompanying strategy, do not drive financial performance;
- Sustainability initiatives by corporations appear to drive better financial performance because they help manage risk better, increase operational efficiency, and drive innovation; and
- Targeting and managing for a low-carbon future improves financial performance.

It may be helpful to distinguish between sustainability frameworks and sustainability standards. They are actually complementary and should be used together.

"Frameworks provide principles-based guidance on how information is structured, how it is prepared, and what broad topics are covered. Meanwhile, standards provide specific, detailed, and replicable requirements for what should be reported for each topic, including metrics. Standards make frameworks actionable, ensuring comparable, consistent, and reliable disclosure."[22]

Heightened scrutiny on greenwashing

Greenwashing is an area of great focus for regulators and the public. The UK Treasury announced in June 2021 a task force to prevent greenwashing so that investors and consumers can make more informed decisions.[23] Anti-greenwashing principles are part of the EU's green taxonomy. In the US, the SEC is pursuing material gaps and inconsistencies in company ESG disclosures.

In-house legal and compliance professionals can help ensure these current best practices for your ESG disclosures and reports:

- Provide the highest-possible level of clarity and completeness;
- Make disclosures easily accessible to stakeholders online;
- Confirm that your employees are aware of the organization's ESG reporting;
- Ensure methodological consistency over time;
- Carefully monitor outgoing content and make all assumptions clear;
- Impose rigorous reviews including at board level; and
- Establish an owner for all ESG statements.

The value of data and other considerations in ESG strategy and reporting

The challenge for stakeholders, including regulatory agencies, is that what is measured and reported is often different, in content and presentation, from one organization to the next. Government officials and investors alike complain that reports don't provide adequate detail expected on climate- and social-related issues. This makes ESG ratings of companies by the most-respected ratings organizations valuable, more reliable, assurance of reports. The data is clearly far harder to find for privately-held companies.

However, differing methodologies mean that even the top ratings agencies (e.g., MSCI and Sustainalytics) may end up with quite different ratings for the same company. To get more granular, these agencies offer hundreds of rating products that delve into specific areas of interest.

Data strategy and tech optimization are increasingly important components of a company's robust ESG program. The systems and methodologies for collecting ESG data are diverse and highly complex. Some companies are moving towards collecting and storing ESG data in isolated files rather than integrated throughout the business. This may prove risky.

Many standard-setting organizations are hoping they will figure out how to harmonize data digitally. As ESG government policies take force globally, companies that have an ability to gather and integrate quality data to help ensure clear and consistent, trackable reporting will have a notable advantage.

ESG regulation is multiplying, causing more involvement of legal

While investors began the sustainability trend, more and more governments, agencies, and associations have joined the rallying call for more and better ESG performance.

All organizations, especially stock exchange-listed companies, are under increased pressure to comply with ESG laws and reporting standards. They are also expected to show their stakeholders (investors, customers, employees, regulators, suppliers, wider communities) that they sincerely care. ESG goals must be woven into the values and the fabric of the business.

Demonstration of commitment to ESG extends from the board all the way through your organization's supply chain, and encompasses new and ongoing development and offering of products and services.

Globally, regulations are moving from soft to hard law on ESG, reflecting the pervasive recognition of climate risk as financial risk.

Part 3: The general counsel's evolving role in ESG

Former GE global CEO and GE general counsel, Alex Dimitrief, said in January 2021:

> *"Legal, compliance and enterprise risk leaders are positioned to play a vitally important role – because of the breadth of your enterprise knowledge, your advocacy and influence skills and your facility in devising and tracking sensible metrics that will effectively measure and reflect a company's progress toward a robust ESG culture."*[24]

The corporate legal and/or compliance leader's role in ESG continues to vary greatly across companies and institutions. The roles the general counsel and chief compliance officer play are as wide-ranging as their companies'

ESG strategy and metrics. In 2020, I saw legal departments fulfilling the important task of helping pull the disparate pieces of evidence together from around the company to begin cohesive ESG reporting.

In talking with many in-house legal and compliance leaders over the last two years, it's clear that ESG roles and responsibilities continue to vary widely from one enterprise to the next. Clarifying your role will be a work in progress for a few years as the ESG field rapidly changes and eventually matures. The corporate legal chief is rarely responsible for ESG, but many are directly connected due to having responsibility for ethics, for example, or litigation or government affairs – and of course, legal risk management.

Some general counsel choose their roles for advocacy as they gain a greater understanding of ESG aspects relevant to their business, many of which have not only a legal or regulatory angle, but an operational one. These typically choose their advocacy themes after clarifying with top executives and stakeholders their ESG priorities.

While I spent some years encouraging general counsel to take a role in reputational risk and advocacy on these issues, today I rarely need to encourage the GC and legal team to get involved in ESG. With their reach across all organizational functions, their diverse skillset and extensive training in ethics, they are already involved.

Governance as starting point

Governance in ESG may be the first point of entry for general counsel into ESG, since they are well-versed in this area. In-house leaders in the services sector, for example, may not fully understand the E and face a learning curve. Most have excellent experience with interpreting and implementing new regulation.

General counsel often say that ESG is important and is a board priority, but that their company is still struggling to find a coordinated and centralized ESG approach. Educating the board on other companies' approaches and helping them to prioritize is another important area for the general counsel.

How the GC fits into your company's ESG structure

As you read the above, many of you may be thinking, "What structure?" If you're confused about how ESG is structured in your organization, you are not alone. It's a real challenge to find an effective approach given the multiple disciplines involved and frequently changing facets of ESG rating frameworks.

Remember how data privacy and cybersecurity used to be found in all different places in the organization, and how today the structure and accountabilities are usually very clear.

Working within multi-disciplinary ESG groups

In-house legal leaders often help develop and implement the enterprise sustainability strategy as part of a multi-disciplinary group. Corporate counsel's unique bird's-eye view of all organizational practices is appreciated, and assists in identifying potential risk areas.

During the first 18 months of the pandemic, our research found that general counsel have been more involved in their company's big strategic decisions than in the past. A part of this is identifying and evaluating ESG implications of those decisions. Some of these decisions carry both opportunities and risks. You can help identify the legal implications the decisions may raise and spotlight potential links to other risks.

To do this effectively, the general counsel should know:

- Who is influencing various elements of ESG in different functions;
- How the reporting is gathered; and
- Whether it accurately aligns with the company's stated ESG objectives.

This requires knowledge of your company's ESG strategy, where your data will be collected, and how it is reported. It can be very helpful to download the various approaches and elements, including in company sustainability reports (Andersons, Kingfisher and Accenture's reports give diverse examples).

General counsel tell me that it very much helps to talk with peers in their own and other industry sectors, to gain new ideas on what they may have missed. This also helps an organization narrow its focus to the highest priorities at present and on the horizon.

> *"The complexities of a growing, global business will be mirrored in its ESG program. To manage this, ESG should be ingrained within the business model and organizational culture – it should not reside within a single function, but all throughout the organization. Sustainability goals should be embedded into the company's strategic business plan. As legal leaders, we can encourage a culture that values ESG and that recognizes our individual responsibility in contributing to a collectively robust ESG program."*[25]

ESG implications for acquisitions, supply chain management, and more

> *"Two-thirds of the average company's environment, social, and governance footprint lies with suppliers."*[26]

General counsel should consider the potential risks arising from corporate inaction related to strategic ESG business decisions. For example, for mergers and acquisitions, you can require that the due diligence process takes ESG into account.

Supply chain and procurement is now a very important area where corporate counsel are expected to understand and contribute views to identify and mitigate ESG risks and opportunities across the supply chain. This includes suppliers' greenhouse gas emissions and also workforce elements such as modern slavery, where global trade sanctions may be a major risk.

Materiality assessment

The general counsel should contribute to the company's materiality assessment, a key aspect of determining ESG strategy and understanding what your metrics and reporting should convey. How your organization decides what's material for stakeholders is required to develop and implement a cohesive, convincing, data-based ESG story that is data-based.

Being a part of the materiality assessment gives the general counsel and her legal team the opportunity to:

- Provide input on the measures that are being considered to demonstrate ESG performance;
- Participate in decisions on how the data to arrive at those measures will be collected and reported; and
- Make sure that various sources of these measures provide data that is aligned and does not potentially contradict the other.

Various websites provide tools to help your organization create its materiality map and assessment. We refer to these in part three.

The legal and compliance leader's role in ESG reporting

Corporate legal and compliance leaders must be involved enough in an organization's ESG strategy and implementation to help the company develop and define parameters around its reporting, both in general and specific terms. If ESG reports create liabilities or damage the company's reputation, it's likely that the legal and compliance functions will be among those held responsible.

Tenneco Chief ESG officer and SVP, Kim Yapchai, underscores the importance of ensuring regulatory compliance and continuity in companies' ESG reports. Yapchai writes:

> *"Both regulators and investors are concerned about greenwashing and expect more precise reporting metrics. Your critical perspective will be important to evaluate whether disclosures are tied to effective data and controls or whether cautionary or clarifying language is needed."*[27]

General counsel know that ESG cannot be an after-the-fact regulatory and compliance concern for the legal team without prior involvement. Last-minute reviews increase the likelihood of incomplete or misaligned ESG disclosures that can expose the legal chief and the company to significant risks – including litigation, regulatory inquiries, and reputational damage. It also under-leverages the key competencies that experienced counsel can bring to the table.

Who has accountability for ESG reporting?

While there seems to be a consensus that accountability for reporting belongs to the board of directors, accountability over the day-to-day management and oversight on ESG is still unclear in many enterprises. ESG strategy and reporting elements are frequently spread across many organizational functions. This makes it very hard to monitor and control risks of greenwashing, especially for a global company. Misaligned or contradictory ESG reports can raise serious problems.

This disjointed approach is understandable and also considered increasingly risky as regulations and public opinion focus on accurate and meaningful demonstration of ESG performance. The general counsel can help clarify the decision-making process and accountabilities.

Pressure points for corporate legal leaders

The Rock Center for Corporate Governance at Stanford University shared its working paper called *The General Counsel View of ESG Risk* in September 2021,[28] reporting on interviews with 70 general counsel in September 2021. The respondents represent diverse industries and 75 percent have >$1bn in revenue. Findings include:

- More than 75 percent of GCs have faced pressure to grow ESG efforts in the past three years;
- Nearly half (48 percent) say the greatest source of pressure for companies is their employees;
- Following employees, investors are second (44 percent), customers (41 percent), advocacy groups (33 percent) and ESG ratings agencies (24 percent);
- General counsel respondents say their companies are most often pressured to invest more money in the diversity, equity, and inclusion part of ESG; and
- Respondents are also worried that disclosing ESG data might increase legal and regulatory risk.

Part 4: Setting priorities and structure for ESG in legal

> *"In the transition to net zero we will need to pass through many shades of brown to shades of green."*[29]

This is how Larry Fink, in his chairman's letter of March 2022, describes the journey to net zero. Add the social and governance pieces to the complexity of environmental action and one sees why general counsel find it difficult to set priorities.

Jennifer Wagner, EVP, corporate affairs and sustainability at Kirkland Lake Gold, explains:

> *"ESG strategy is never one-size-fits-all, but rather tailored to a company's unique sector, regional operations, and stakeholder base. The sweet spot is finding ESG objectives that align with business objectives."*[30]

If the general counsel actively helps your organization set priorities, that will then guide your focus – at least for the coming 12 months or so. The legal function cannot possibly take on all aspects at once or effectively predict new ESG risks. The current ESG noise from everywhere can be a wasteful distraction.

Tenneco's chief ESG officer and former compliance head, Kim Yapchai, states:

> *"ESG is different for each company – there's not one simple definition. I see*

that as a great opportunity, with the flexibility to partner with our business to determine what's most important to our stakeholders."[31]

Understanding your stakeholders' ESG interests

As you help your organization define material ESG factors, it's important to determine your primary stakeholders. What concerns them most? What kind of ESG information do they seek? These answers will inform the ESG reporting frameworks and standards you adopt for your disclosures. If your primary stakeholders are investors, your focus might be on ESG issues that most directly impact the company's financial value and use for your reporting an investor-focused standard such as SASB, the Task Force on Climate-Related Financial Disclosures (TCFD) or the Global ESG Benchmark for Real Assets (GRESB).

If you are subject to regulation such as the EU's upcoming Corporate Sustainability Reporting Directive, you will need to consider "double materiality". It's recommended to then choose a broad scope ESG reporting framework, such as the UN Sustainable Development Goals (SDGs), the Global Reporting Initiative (GRI). or the World Economic Forum's Stakeholder Capitalism Metrics.

Network with your peers on ESG

By networking with peers, you can gain ideas and insights from those who are quite advanced with their ESG implementation after years of refining a program, as well as from those that are still determining their ESG strategy and finding their way. Sharing ideas and practices with peers may be more useful to you than attending presentations on fast-changing ESG trends.

There's no easy roadmap to follow, but there are many tools and approaches to help you set priorities and make progress. Yapchai recommends:

"You can't be all things to all people. What matters the most to you? If you start off with what makes the most sense for your company, it's easier to find small steps that create momentum to move forward. It's a journey without a clear finish line."[32]

What will be your company's ESG story?

Daragh Fagan, former group GC and corporate secretary of FTSE 100 Rentokil Initial, provides valuable advice:

> *"Satisfying diverse stakeholders in different regions is a challenging task for multinational companies. However, it is possible to address key local ESG issues while simultaneously tackling global ones that affect your whole supply chain. You must decide what activities to prioritize, communicate these effectively and ultimately accept that you won't always be able to please everyone."*[33]

As stated above, you should participate in developing your company's distinct definition of its environmental, social, and governance areas of focus. As general counsel, you can help ensure that once your company determines its ESG "story", it will be articulated effectively, with data collection that can report progress.

Distance yourself from the reactive phase of ESG which can be overwhelming and unproductive (e.g., focusing on improving overall ratings, etc.). As Fagan says, focus on the issues that the company has decided are business mission-critical. Otherwise, ESG may become more of a promotional exercise, exposing you to greenwashing and credibility risks, both externally and internally.

There's no need to take on the world and solve all the UN Sustainable Development Goals (SDGs) – you can choose if you wish to follow a few of the SDGs. MSCI also has a materiality map with a helpful structure to prioritize what is material for your industry.[34]

Practices for the legal team

In-house legal and compliance professionals can help ensure these best practices for their organization's ESG disclosures and reports:

- Provide the highest-possible level of clarity and completeness;
- Make disclosures easily accessible to stakeholders online;
- Confirm that your employees are aware of the organization's ESG reporting;
- Ensure methodological consistency and alignment of reports over time;
- Carefully monitor outgoing content and make all assumptions clear;
- Impose rigorous reviews including at the board level;
- Establish an owner for every ESG statement.

ESG requires professionals that connect various actions of different parts of the organization to ensure continuity. For example, legal leaders are usually far more aware than business leaders of the company's litigation strategy. If there are aspects of the litigation strategy that may conflict with your company's ESG positioning, you should raise the issues and recommend ways to mitigate.

How much ESG reporting is enough, and who makes that decision?

The media reports examples of the rigor of ESG regulatory enforcement coming from the SEC, the UK, and the German regulatory agencies. The court of public opinion is also vocal. News of "bad actors" in ESG areas can drive down customer and employee confidence and the company's share price.

While we hope for streamlined regulation eventually, the most advanced regulation today is in the EU. Its requests require detailed third-party confirmation of report validity and also require the company to ensure that suppliers are taking similar action.

The enormous emphasis on measuring and reporting (or disclosures, in the narrower sense) underscores the necessity to decide how your company measures and reports on performance against ESG strategy. This is where data gathering, analysis and integration plays a huge role, as discussed in part two.

Many general counsel start by measuring all the company's existing initiatives that fall into the E, S, and G categories. SASB provides some examples as a guide.[35]

Blockchain and artificial intelligence hold promise for streamlining ESG reporting but the lion's share of companies are not actively harnessing these methods for that purpose yet. Many organizations are already using automation and digitalization to integrate their data more effectively. Listed companies are paying more attention to data quality and control, which increasingly presents both a challenge, a risk, and an opportunity in ESG.

Clear and consistent ESG terminology

A global industrial company's general counsel rightly stated at one of our roundtables, "*It's important to give your definition of various ESG terms when discussing it with people outside of your organization, as its meaning can vary greatly across contexts*". In writing this chapter it was astounding to me how broadly the basic definitions and use of ESG terms vary.

Inconsistent ESG data and unclear terminology is an obstacle. Companies in specific sectors are wise to agree to similar terminology so that there is more clarity for diverse stakeholders. Some trade associations are spearheading those efforts and making good progress. Help ensure that your ESG terminology is consistent across the enterprise. It will be required to enable your organization to harness technology and data integration to streamline and standardize your ESG reporting.

Expected developments in ESG reporting

Development of a common global system of frameworks and taxonomies that surpasses national regulatory boundaries is a realistic expectation – but a long way away. When we get there, it will make the reporting process more efficient.

The EU Taxonomy Regulation established an EU-wide framework to provide businesses and investors with a common language to determine how environmentally sustainable economic activities are.[36] Their goal is to speed behavioral change, to help investors and consumers make more informed decisions.

Many feel that this EU regulation will provide a benchmark for ESG standards in other countries, similar to the standard that GDPR set for many countries on data privacy regulation. The EU is also likely to bring its focus on ESG to the table when discussing trade and other multilateral agreements, which gives an incentive to countries they trade with to regulate ESG themselves.

The EU Taxonomy Regulation is complex and multi-faceted and is taking effect as follows:

- 1 January 2022: For the environmental objectives of climate change mitigation and climate change adaptation.
- 1 January 2023: Other environmental objectives (sustainable use and protection of water and marine resources; the transition to a circular economy; pollution prevention and control; and the protection and restoration of biodiversity and ecosystems).

Task Force on Climate-Related Financial Disclosures

General counsel should make every effort to inform their C-suite and board about the TCFD reporting framework and the current emphasis on it.

In June 2021, finance ministers of the G7 called for making disclosure of climate-related financial risks compulsory for companies and endorsed the framework of the Task Force on Climate-Related Financial Disclosures (TCFD), chaired by Michael Bloomberg. The majority of the world's largest public companies now report along TCFD guidelines, according to the TCFD's 2021 Status Report.[37]

The European Union has incorporated TCFD recommendations into its Taxonomy Regulation, and the UK in November 2020 announced its plans to make disclosure requirements mandatory by 2025, in alignment with the TCFD.[38]

As of 2021, nearly 600 individual firms with a combined $54 trillion in assets under management and representing 80 percent of global industrial emissions have joined Climate Action 100+, an initiative urging companies to implement the recommendations of the TCFD.[39]

What next?

As mentioned at the start of this chapter, it's nearly impossible for your legal team to stay updated on the massive, constantly-changing ESG space. You might try the Big Four's updates on their websites, but ESG news varies widely by industry as well as by ESG framework and standards. And then one must consider workplace issues and differing governance standards by jurisdiction. It's likely to be 2025 before the clouds clear and the noise becomes reasonable. Much of that clarity will come from regulation, which will also evolve.

For now, it's clear that priorities count, and general counsel must contribute and continually revise based on new developments significant to their company's business. General counsel have successfully weathered many major changes in global regulation in the 21st century already – from the General Data Privacy Act to Sarbanes Oxley in the US, to anti-corruption regulation in many countries. There is no question you can do the same with ESG, as you contribute to reducing climate change – making the planet and your company a better place.

References

1 Global Counsel Leaders Benchmark Report, 2020.

2 www.bloomberg.com/company/press/esg-may-surpass-41-trillion-assets-in-2022-but-not-without-challenges-finds-bloomberg-intelligence/

3 'ESG fund fees, How to charge more', *The Economist*, July 21, 2022 – special report: ESG Investing: A Broken Idea.

4 www.gsb.stanford.edu/faculty-research/publications/general-counsel-view-esg-risk

5 www.bloomberg.com/company/press/esg-may-surpass-41-trillion-assets-in-2022-but-not-without-challenges-finds-bloomberg-intelligence/ – 24 Jan 2022.

6 Discussed in part two, most regulation considers double materiality: both the company's own actions to reduce its negative impact on ESG issues and the impact of external ESG events on the company's projected performance.

7 https://hbr.org/2022/08/esg-investing-isnt-designed-to-save-the-planet

8 https://www.pwc.co.uk/human-resource-services/assets/pdfs/environmental-social-governance-exec-pay-report.pdf

9 www.ft.com/content/609eae5e-1576-4081-9340-5d5001b5b02e

10 www.ga-institute.com/

11 http://media-publications.bcg.com/france/pulse-of-the-fashion-industry2019.pdf

12 https://web-assets.bcg.com/27/f3/794284e7437d99a71d625caf589f/consumers-adaptation-to-sustainability-in-fashion.pdf

13 www.firstinsight.com/press-releases/first-insight-finds-expectations-for-sustainable-retail-practices-growing-with-the-rise-of-gen-z-shoppers

14 *Report on ESG for Corporate Legal & Compliance Leaders*, Jan 2022, Global Counsel Leaders, https://globalcounselleaders.com/gcl-2022-esg-report, Preface.

15 https://corporatefinanceinstitute.com/resources/knowledge/other/esg-environmental-social-governance/

16 Commentary by Carmen Nuzzo: https://globalcounselleaders.com/gcl-2022-esg-report, p.47.

17 Lex Mundi 2022 Summit Report, Stakeholder Governance and General Counsel, www.lexmundi-summit2022.com/.

18 www.blackrock.com/us/individual/2022-larry-fink-ceo-letter

19 Lex Mundi 2022 Summit Report, Stakeholder Governance and General Counsel, www.lexmundi-summit2022.com/.

20 *Report on ESG for Corporate Legal & Compliance Leaders*, Jan 2022, Global Counsel Leaders, https://globalcounselleaders.com/gcl-2022-esg-report, Preface.

21 www.stern.nyu.edu/experience-stern/faculty-research/new-meta-analysis-nyu-stern-center-sustainable-business-and-rockefeller-asset-management-finds-esg

22 www.sasb.org/about/sasb-and-other-esg-frameworks/

23 https://www.gov.uk/government/news/new-independent-group-to-help-tackle-greenwashing

24 *Global Counsel Leaders' 2021 Comprehensive Report on ESG Issues for Corporate Legal and Compliance Leaders*, Globalcounselleaders.com, Preface.

25 Andrea Wood, Chief Legal and Governance Officer at TELUS, Vancouver, Canada, *Global Counsel Leaders' Mid-Year Report on ESG Issues for Corporate Legal and Compliance Leaders*, July 2021.

26 Mckinsey.com, *Buying into a More Sustainable Value Chain*, 9-22-21.

27 *Global Counsel Leaders' 2022 Comprehensive Report on ESG Issues for Corporate Legal and Compliance Leaders*, Globalcounselleaders.com, Commentary.

28 https://papers.ssrn.com/sol3/papers.cfm?abstract_id=3923913

29 www.blackrock.com/corporate/investor-relations/larry-fink-chairmans-letter

30 *Mid-year 2021 ESG Report for Corporate Legal & Compliance Leaders*, GlobalCounselLeaders.com.

31 *Global Counsel Leaders' 2022 Comprehensive Report on ESG Issues for Corporate Legal and Compliance Leaders*, Globalcounselleaders.com, Commentary.

32 *Ibid.*

33 *2022 ESG Report for Corporate Legal and Compliance Leaders*, Global Counsel Leaders.

34 www.msci.com/our-solutions/esg-investing/esg-industry-materiality-map

35 https://www.sasb.org

36 https://finance.ec.europa.eu/sustainable-finance/tools-and-standards/eu-taxonomy-sustainable-activities_en#:~:text=What%20is%20the%20EU%20taxonomy,implement%20the%20European%20green%20deal

37 www.fsb-tcfd.org/

38 https://www.gov.uk/government/publications/uk-joint-regulator-and-government-tcfd-taskforce-interim-report-and-roadmap

39 https://www.climateaction100.org/progress/progress-update/

Chapter 11: Quantifying value creation in legal departments – showing the income side of legal work

By Christoph H. Vaagt, founder and managing partner, Law Firm Change Consultants

One approach that some corporate legal departments are taking to increase the value of their services requires a culture change. The legal department makes a valuable contribution to the business – not only by driving activity through an ever-growing number of legal requirements and actions to protect the business from risk, but also in the form of quantifiable financial contributions. These contributions, if ever reflected on a legal department's balance sheet or business plan, would be enormous.

The financial value of the legal department has always been difficult to measure. With increasing demands for cost efficiency, the other side of the balance sheet, i.e., revenue, should also become the focus of the legal department. It will become clear that the legal department should no longer be viewed as a cost center, but as a profit center.

Old versus new world of legal departments

Traditionally, the primary role of in-house counsel was risk mitigation. The fundamental criterion for success was ensuring that their employer was legally compliant. Traditional definitions of value are typically customer-focused – innovative, pragmatic, and easy to manage.

Regulatory design and response is also a traditional focus of legal departments. In terms of financial performance, it's mostly about managing legal costs with the goal of making them cost less over time. Rarely is it about helping the company generate revenue on transactions or new product development.

The new normal for legal departments

Legal departments have come under increasing scrutiny from finance and procurement departments over the past 15 years. Corporate counsel have been pressured to streamline their processes and justify capacity. Doing more with less became the credo. Like every other department in the company, legal departments must submit a plan. This planning almost always concerns only the cost side and assumes that the "revenue side" either does not exist or is not quantifiable. Almost all KPIs are therefore cost-oriented. Revenues in this sense are only those that have been generated by cost savings.

The traditional view is that the legal department "supports" the activities of the corporate departments (R&D, production, marketing, sales) that have traditionally been actively involved in value creation; the focus of the company, whether service delivery or production. These departments have to work within the legal framework, and the prevailing view is that there is a legal function for this. It is either a matter of reviewing and revising contracts, providing legal advice in between to clarify the scope of action of the players, or defending against lawsuits or enforcing one's own claims through negotiations or lawsuits.

But isn't there revenue on the credit side of the balance sheet or on the revenue side of the department's business plan? My hypothesis is that these are as easy (or difficult) to quantify as any other projected revenue for the other departments and can be calculated quite accurately after the fact.

For some years now, there have been proposals and checklists (ACC, Practical Law Institute), but most of them refer to typical cases where the claim is obvious (so-called affirmative recovery programs) because it arises from law (damages), contract (e.g., insurance), or regulatory notice (e.g., finding of illegal antitrust conduct).

In some areas of law, this already leads to clear business cases, e.g., in the area of patents held by a company. These represent quantifiable legal positions that can, for example, lead to revenue in the form of licenses or infringements by competitors, damages, etc. Patents, trademarks, etc. are therefore described in financial terms in due diligences when selling companies.

Generally, in M&A transactions, all legal risks are quantified and, in this case, usually realized as a price premium/discount or provided with guarantees.

However, most legal issues have financial implications. It is simply a matter of examining the legal transactions for their economic potential. Two types of financial impact arise – increases in value that lead directly to monetary income, or indirectly to income that can be recognized in the balance sheet. The latter are at least partly attributable to the value added by the legal department.

Direct income-generating activities

The following revenue generating opportunities are traditionally used:

1. *Trade secret lawsuits.* A core business function, trade secret lawsuits often have an international component that makes them difficult and expensive to pursue.
2. *Contractual claims.* A factor to consider is the size and nature of the opposing organization. Some of DuPont's early lawsuits were against electric utilities, which minimized the risk of a bad reputation and the appearance of a bully.
3. *Insurance.* Insurance coverage disputes are common, but insurance companies have deep pockets. Litigation funding levels the playing field. Lawsuits against insurance companies have the added benefit of low reputational risk.
4. *Tort claims.* Proving wrongful interference with business operations can be time-consuming and expensive, but improves the bottom line in several ways – not only through financial recovery, but also by stopping the harmful activity.
5. *Antitrust.* Not only is ensuring fair competition critical to the company's business, but antitrust judgments in US federal courts often provide for treble damages, which can make these claims particularly lucrative. In Europe, damages must be directly related to the economic impact of the cause, but are relatively easy to enforce because the claim has previously been established by the authorities.

Very rarely, some companies talk about direct revenue generation, e.g., by offering a work product of the legal department like "white legal content" selling it to interested parties without reference to the authors.

Indirect value contributions of the legal department – measure in order to prove value

Indirect value contributions are those that avoid or reduce costs and generate revenue increases. They are much more difficult to collect and evaluate. Without this, however, the real value of the legal department's activities does not become clear, especially in a world where only what can be quantified counts, while the value of intangible contributions or those that defy quantifiability does not count in the world of (business) management.

1. They are mainly found in contract drafting, where the legal department supports other business units. Typically, the department then realizes a "deal" assigned to the department as a success that results in bonuses for employees and an increase in revenue for the entire company, but not a corresponding "booking" in the legal department in terms of costs saved or an increase in the revenue/profit potential of the corporate project in the future. This is in contrast to departments such as sales, where, for example, "network/alliance sales" by vendors are recognized for enabling potential sales that are then actually realized by other departments/employees. Or employees who patent an invention and receive employee compensation or similar for it, even regardless of whether the invention can ever be monetized or leads to competitive improvements in products. In my opinion, the same claims are comparable to what lawyers do. Lawyers directly or indirectly ensure the optimization of value creation in companies.
2. Negotiation of cost risk by the legal department can lead to millions of dollars in savings over time, a risk that the negotiating sales unit may not have included in the contract, contributing to cost avoidance or revenue generation.
3. Economic issues also play a role in considering which method to use to realize damages in antitrust damages cases. It has a decisive impact on the "business case" of such a case. Litigation costs can run into the millions if appropriate lawyers and economists are used; alternative dispute resolution options may be less expensive. Ultimately, the legal department decides which path makes more sense and thus has a direct influence on the resulting revenue.
4. Monitoring trends in legislation and case law and influencing them is also one of the areas in which new opportunities for realizing revenue/profit potential, on the one hand, and avoiding risk, on the other, arise. Evaluating these developments will be the task of a proactively managed legal department in the future.
5. Far more difficult to quantify are the contributions resulting from training courses, legal briefings, and instructions. Again, the ultimate question is what economic value is at stake, what would be at stake in alternative behavior, and how the legal department helps to influence that. Even a one percent influence on a decision that moves billions is to their credit – if the legal department were a sales team, they would fight for every percentage point.

6. Companies that act in a value-oriented manner are more successful economically. One of the most important levers for this is the continuous training of managers and techniques to become "legally astute managers"[1] because their understanding of law as a resource and not just a constraint stimulates them to do better business. Corporate returns that realize five percent return on sales instead of four percent, that is significant profit potential, and legal departments would have a significant part in realizing it through such a program.
7. Compliance programs that provide not only a minimum of guidance on the legal framework but also concrete instructions for action can save many billions. As early as the 1970s, for example, Volkswagen was sentenced to pay damages in the US for failing to comply with emission standards for vehicle engines in California. Engine development always straddles the line between what is still legal and what is illegal in terms of emissions, as this has a direct impact on fuel consumption or fuel economy. A compliance program that would have ensured that technicians were never allowed to make decisions about thermal insulation windows without legal support would have saved the VW Group 32 billion euros since 2015.

Necessary cultural change

The cultural change necessary for this has actually been underway for a long time – with the introduction of KPIs, lawyers in legal departments have learned to align their actions with economic data. Already, 56 percent of CFOs surveyed (see Burford Study 2021) answered in the affirmative to the question of whether legal departments should have economic goals (44 percent against).[2] However, in order to not only be better positioned in the company than the cost centers, but to actually insist on considering the economic consequences of their actions, mapping them in business plans, and realizing them, lawyers will have to act much more commercially than they have in the past. There is much evidence to suggest that this is difficult for lawyers, even though a new generation is emerging to deal with it.

To begin the process of realignment, it is helpful to have a strategic process that challenges the department's core assumptions and makes new things possible. Change always begins with a clear inventory. This includes, for example:

- Creating a targeted analysis to examine the department's strengths, weaknesses, opportunities, and threats (SWOT analysis). If the legal department uses metrics to track the legal department's performance, analyzing those metrics can be helpful in conducting a SWOT analysis or other assessment of the department.

- Defining short- and long-term goals that support the legal department's mission. Some legal departments go beyond this step and create business plans for the legal department.
- Developing the legal department's budget on both the cost and revenue sides and deciding if and where budget adjustments are appropriate, how the department contributes directly or indirectly to the bottom line, what new projects to fund, and reviewing the legal department's culture and considering adjustments in that regard, that legal staff have a solid understanding of the economic impact of their legal advice and are trained in economic evaluation, and that there is no disconnect between the legal department and other corporate departments that results in staff avoiding consulting the legal department or ignoring the legal department's direction.

This may include establishing a legal department operations management function. This means better managing the legal department itself, i.e., aligning it with goals, monitoring development progress, making corrections, and constantly striving for optimization. Without this function, the legal department could quickly fall back into the old routine of mainly doing casework and caring less about ignoring the ever-increasing demands that characterize the corporate world.

The biggest challenge is to change the perception of the legal department. To do this, the head of the legal department in particular, but all in-house counsel as well, must constantly pay attention to how they are viewed internally. So the question they have to ask themselves is, first and foremost, how can we help the company make money or make more money through our legal advice and our legal knowledge of processes and developments. Knowing that a dollar of cost to the sales department typically generates $30 of revenue, we can also assume for the legal department that the ratio of one to 30 should be applied to the legal department's costs. So the legal department needs to collect 30 times its cost budget. This only sounds good if there is a clear focus on making economic contributions and these are quantified. If a legal department reviews its files for the last several months from the standpoint of the economic impact of every legal tip, advice, or contract, it will discover an incredible amount of economic contributions it has made through its legal services. Usually, however, the economic value was not recorded at the time of service. What is critical in each case is the need to financially record these realized or realizable value contributions.

Only when in-house lawyers can see in quantified form what contributions they have made, or perhaps could have made, will it become clear to all lawyers how great the impact of their work is on the economic success of the company.

Getting this change process right will be the biggest challenge for in-house counsel in the coming years.

References

1 Constance E Bagley, *Winning Legally: How Managers Can Use the Law to Create Value, Marshal Resources, and Manage Risk*, Harvard Business Review Press, 2005.

2 https://www.burfordcapital.com/insights/insights-container/2021-legal-asset-report/

Chapter 12:

Managing change in a legal department – introduction of a contract management system

By Wolf-Peter Gross, management consultant, Law Firm Change Consultants

Legal departments are basically subject to the same dynamics of change as other organizations or organizational units. At the same time, they have significant peculiarities. These are essentially the result of the particular professional self-image of lawyers, as well as the variety of roles ranging from salaried employee on the one hand and professional on the other. In addition, there are the dimensions of staff, stakeholders of change, such as operative units, functional areas, management or the company itself, which are affected by change. This must be considered in change processes if they are to be successful.

Change in general

Change is easy if "the old comes in the garment of the new".[1] Dealing with the resistance of individuals as well as organizations is the linchpin of change projects. In general, humans find it difficult to change something in their lives. We already know what provides us with a feeling of familiarity and security – even if they can cognitively grasp the price we pay for remaining in the familiar situation. The known seems better than anything unknown. Humans know their way around it, have learned their survival techniques – and no one can truly guarantee them that the new will be better; after all, it could get worse! Humans tend to imagine the worst. We are very good at anticipating risks and dangers and getting ready for them. Decision psychology shows in impressive experiments that people are more receptive to losses than to gains. The strategy of sticking with the tried and tested seems to be deeply rooted in developmental history. Sticking to the known offers more survival advantages than taking risks.

As brain research has shown, there is a range of individual willingness to change, which is partly genetically predetermined and partly strengthened by socialization. Accordingly, groups of people can be observed in change projects, which generally can be divided into 10-15 percent drivers, 35-40 percent passive protagonists, 35-40 percent wait-and-see sceptics and

10-15 percent refusers. Experience shows that the proportion of sceptics is somewhat higher in legal departments, which can be attributed to the professional socialization of the legal profession. They are in a very unique position to identify risks and develop strategies to avoid them.

Another characteristic of change processes is that everyone experiences emotional phases that are defined by corresponding behavioral patterns.

Kubler-Ross Change Curve, adapted from Optima Training (UK) Limited.

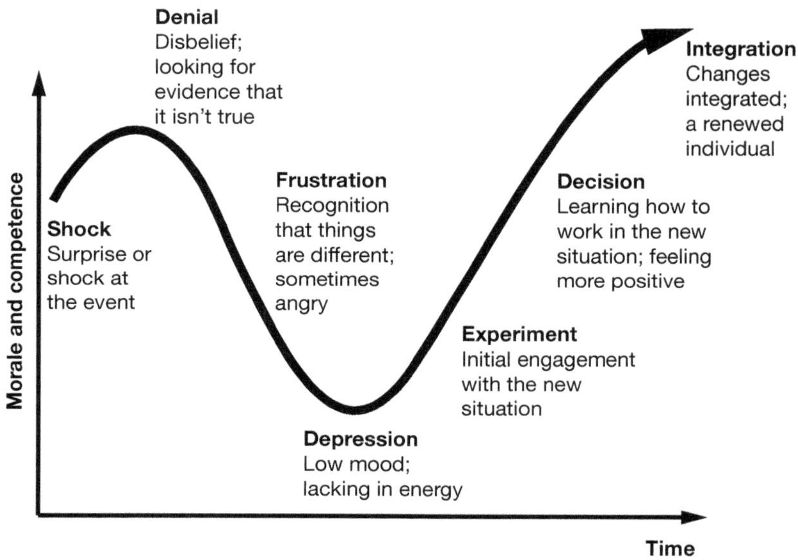

It is fundamental to recognize and accept these emotional phases, which have been sufficiently researched by sociologists. Lawyers in particular tend to seek out the factual level and suppress the emotional side. In their own affairs, however (i.e., when it comes to one's own change), emotions play the central role. It is important to work with these emotions in order to implement change projects successfully. The two pieces of bad news are:

- There is no shortcut from the state of denial to positive acceptance; and
- The change curve occurs with a time lag; typically the masterminds and initiators of change are emotionally at a different stage than the circle of early initiates, let alone the rest of the employees.

This has implications for communication and the design of the change process. People adapt to change at their own pace. Understanding and agreeing takes time, and even if the change protagonists wish otherwise, a "once and done" approach is counterproductive. The duration depends on various factors such as the degree of need for change, the attractiveness of the goal, the extent and impact of the change, or the previous change experience of the stakeholders.

Another essential prerequisite for understanding the management of change projects is the change formula: $C = D \times V \times F > R$.[2] The natural resistance to change is so great that the product of the need for change, times its objective, times the first steps in the desired direction, must be greater than the resistance.

The process of change only comes into operation when the why and the purpose of the change are clear. The why results from the initial situation and corresponds to the "dissatisfaction" factor in the change formula. The goal needs to answer the meaningful question of what the purpose of the change is. There is a natural gap between the initial situation and the vision of the change, which needs to be bridged. The description of the task packages as well as the change process, i.e., the architecture of involvement and participation, as well as the first quick wins, are the necessary stabilizers that every change project requires to become viable. Ideally, the project has a motto that inspires and strengthens the sense of unity.

These basic logics of change management apply equally to legal departments. However, in the case of these, further special features must be taken into account.

Change in legal departments

The profession of lawyers is essentially a liberal profession. Independence is a core element. Deeply rooted convictions and values derive from professional autonomy, which shape the self-perception as well as influence structures, behavior, governance, and processes in legal departments. The professionals, most of whom claim to have sovereignty of judgement based on superior expertise and training as decision-makers (continental Europe), are often reserved when third parties formulate different requirements for the effectiveness, quality, or efficiency of their work.

At the same time, a high value orientation is evident, which is expressed in a strong consensus orientation and respect for the professional sphere of the other managers in the company. Since change processes in legal departments almost always have an impact on other company units, the tendency to avoid conflict on one's own account naturally influences the breadth, depth, and speed of change.

Subliminally, other interests are involved, which (often covertly) are defended. The in-house lawyers want to avoid anything that could undermine their authority, reputation, and credibility in the company. Transparency or metrics related to performance or quality standards that could put them in a bad light are often avoided. This is an important obstacle, especially in change projects that are intended to increase the legal department's value contribution to the company. Arguments such as pointing to an allegedly inconsistent numerical basis are typical masking tactics designed to distract from the necessity of the project. In legal departments, change is often referred back to one's own individual performance/willingness to perform, and thus in change projects there is a subliminal fear of not looking good and losing influence that has been gained with great effort.

Case study: Introduction of a case management system

An internationally positioned, family-run logistics company was organized in a highly decentralized way. The operational managers had a high level of decision-making authority. Due to enormous and rapid growth, demands on risk management increased. The CFO, a third-party manager, decided to introduce a contract management system in order to be able to create and maintain a risk register of all contracts. The contract management system was to be administered and controlled by the legal department. The head of the legal department reported to the CFO.

First, the legal department drew up the specifications, which primarily mapped the risk concerns of the corporate group. On this basis, a shortlist of software providers was drawn up. With the help of a decision matrix, a provider was selected to implement the system.

The project met with resistance. First learning: Change begins with the conception of the project. This does not mean that the question of whether or not to introduce a contract management system should be put up for discussion. Rather, the management should have set a framework in which the stakeholders could have brought in their own interests. The specifications should have been written together with those affected by the introduction of a system. In this way, the decentralized units were practically put in front of a fait accompli, since the order had already been placed before they were involved. At this point a change process was set up with the help of external consultants, which enabled permeable communication and involvement of the main stakeholders.

Working- and decision-making structure.

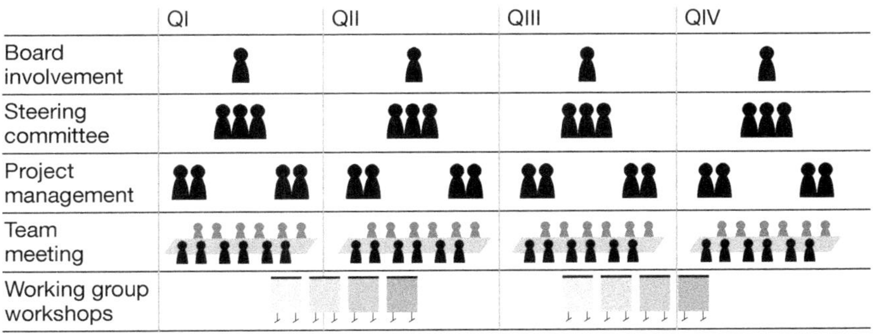

The main reservations were about the transparency that could be created through a contract management system. The operational managers did not want errors or compliance violations to be proven to them. The project management therefore decided to include only new contracts in the system, but not old contracts. Contracts that were up for renewal had to be approved by the contract owners for inclusion in the system.

The second important decision was to make the high-turnover operational managers players in the project, as advisors and ambassadors in the steering committee. In this way, they took on project responsibility and ensured acceptance in their units. This step was also important because the shareholder-managing director and CEO was only behind the project if he got the signal that the decentralized managers were strongly in favor of introducing a contract management system. The board of directors was kept regularly informed of the project's progress as part of the project architecture. The second learning was: involve those who have power, influence, and are affected by the change, and hold them accountable.

The third learning for the project came from the process architecture: a fixed time and communication frame that ensures the participation of the most important stakeholders, a project management that regularly reflects on the progress of the project and intervenes in a corrective way in case of influences or deviations, the securing of support for the project by – in this case – the owners, and the involvement of working groups that were composed of diverse members and worked out important topics such as the authorization concept or the structures for keywording. All these elements were success factors for this project.

The project was underpinned by an agile project management logic that made intermediate steps visible at an early stage, put them up for discussion in sounding groups, and let the feedback flow back into the project.

The change process

The change process can be visualized with the help of the so-called "House of Change", i.e., the need for change is derived from the analysis of the initial situation, the vision is developed in workshops, the work packages for achieving the goals are defined, and a process architecture is developed, which ensures that good decisions about the project can be made.

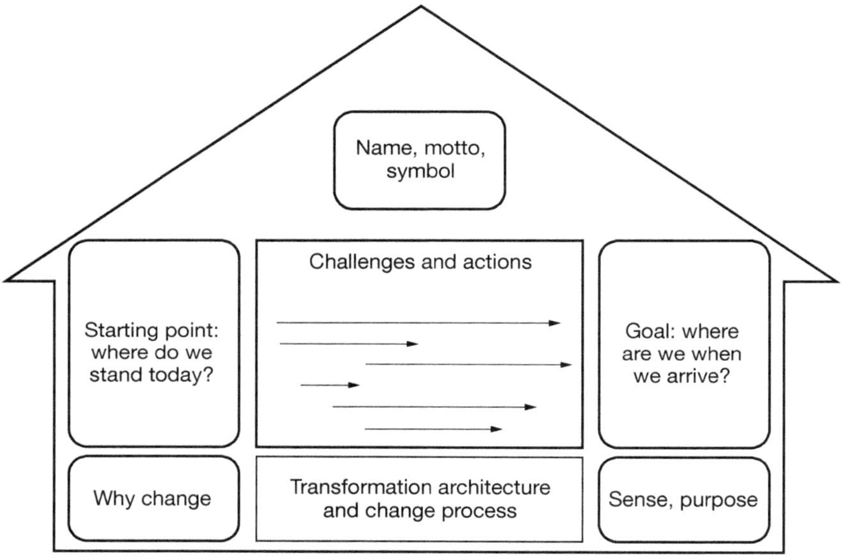

Source: Based on the model of the consulting organisation Beratergruppe Neuwaldegg.

Starting point

In recent years, the pressure on legal departments has increased continuously. This has various reasons.

- Almost all value chains are fragmented and globalized. At the same time, the regulatory framework for entrepreneurial activity is becoming ever tighter. It also plays a role that the legal systems, terminology, views, preconceptions, professional responsibilities, or roles of in-house lawyers or attorneys can differ significantly, depending on whether they are influenced by common law, civil law, or other legal systems. This places high demands on the management, structure, and organization of legal in the company in order to be able to do business safely – one of, if not the main task of the legal management and the legal department. Managerial liability is getting tougher and thus corporate lawyers are moving closer to the CEO and the entire board of directors.

- Competition is becoming more intense and product life cycles shorter. This leads to enormous pressure on those responsible for operations. Goals are becoming increasingly short-term, and it is becoming more and more difficult for managers to influence their attainability. The time pressure thus also affects the legal departments, which have to provide legal advice in the decision-making processes.
- Business life is becoming increasingly legalized and the legal department is becoming more and more involved in compliance and risk management processes. This changes the role of the legal department and demands more resources and competences.
- Cost pressure is constantly increasing. Processes have to be streamlined accordingly, procedures and contracts standardized, and the task portfolio reviewed and adapted.

All these issues, be it pressure on efficiency, dissatisfaction of the legal department's internal clients with the speed of response or lack of solution orientation, compliance incidents, technological developments or digital transformation, changes in internal standards and process flows, or changes in the market or the product and service portfolio lead to pressure for change that has to be managed.

As a rule, legal departments adapt dynamically to minor changes in their environment. Examples include communication, which has evolved from dictated letters to self-written emails or smartphone communication and has increased significantly in speed. Efficiency programs were put in place in response to the finance department's requirement to do more with less.

In other areas, legal departments are finding it harder to change, especially when it comes to responding appropriately to insidious or disruptive developments. The latter are rare. The former are not. They usually result from not looking at key figures, not reflecting on work processes, not talking to the stakeholders and internal clients, or not managing the value contribution. The latently perceived changes in the quality of work, the time wasters due to the late involvement of the legal department, the lack of anchoring legal requirements in the process chains, are accepted or even glossed over, excuses are sought, such as the belief that nothing can be changed anyway. This usually distracts from the real problems, which are perpetuated by the pattern of "close your eyes and get through it".

The need for change is often seen in terms of operational issues – more stringent processes, higher efficiency, improved quality standards, or more professional legal operations management. Strategic changes that affect the business model or the positioning within the company are more difficult. This is because in-house lawyers often do not have a clear understanding of their own business model and the actual levers to increase their contribution to value creation.

The analysis of the starting position requires a detached view with which the positioning and the key figures are prepared. Only in this way the filters of self-perception can be mirrored by an objectified view. Methodological aids are data analysis (evaluation of key figures with a view to effectiveness, efficiency, and profitability), bench marking, stakeholder surveys, which enable an external view on the work of the legal department, SWOT[3] analysis, which in contrast maps the internal perspective of the legal department on the environment, or portfolio analysis with a focus on the value added contribution of the different tasks of the legal department.

Many legal departments have developed a permanent and thus low-threshold mode of adapting to changes based on continuous observation of the environment and evaluation of key performance indicators. In such legal departments, strategy and operational improvement are discussed on an ongoing basis. They are usually healthy at their core; the need for change is accordingly low, unless unforeseen influences arise. Legal departments with a high need for change and a low willingness to change have usually systematically overlooked the warning signs. Others, usually CEO or CFO, then instruct the necessary restructuring.

Goal and vision

A legal department that is strategically or operationally not well positioned and thus not optimally effective in relation to its core business giving legal advice cannot reinvent itself overnight like a phoenix rising from the ashes. It is illusory to strive for a leap evolution. The depth and speed of change in legal departments depends on the degree of their own imagination and confidence in their ability to change things. Against this backdrop, it is often difficult to find a vision that is attractive, i.e., clearly recognizable and underpinned by a comprehensible, resilient value proposition. Such a quality vision, however, is a necessary basis for the possibility of positioning the legal department better in the company and thus becoming more effective.

A typical example is a legal department that is not anchored in the operational process flows and therefore very often has to react, that is in strategic plans or important operational projects of the company not part of the team from the very beginning and has no real access to the deep-seated risks that can arise from high-handedness of operational managers. The level of frustration is high, there is a prevailing feeling of not being recognized in the work, and not being adequately used in the legal department's ability and competences.

The greatest challenge in the necessary change process was in this case to find a vision that was not only externally vis-à-vis the most important stakeholders in the company, but also internally in such a way that the majority of the legal departments team members could identify with it. Resistance was particularly strong because the in-house lawyers, who did good professional work but were not confident in their role as strategic legal advisors and thought leaders, were worried about their professional future in the legal department. It was therefore important, on the one hand, to underpin the vision with a personnel development process that offered a comprehensible and credible opportunity to learn the counselling skills and also to strengthen the individual personality for this purpose, and, on the other hand, to differentiate the task portfolio in such a way that pure professional legal work had a valued place in the second row, quasi behind the scenes.

Often there are fears associated with change that are not openly expressed. Questions like: Will I still be needed? Can I deliver what is described as new? The vision cannot take away these fears; they have to be taken into account in the change process.

Goals and images do not only have to be strategic in nature. They can also include cultural components, especially if the pressure for change results from internal tensions and conflicts. In any case, it is important that the vision provides orientation, creates identity, is SMART,[4] and, above all, attractive. Methodologically helpful for this are methods such as Future Search,[5] vision work,[6] creative techniques such as mind maps or design thinking, analogue forms of work such as the creation of collages, videos or similar, as they enable a more emotional approach and thus ensure congruent values from which the meaning of the change can be derived. The meaning behind the development is just as crucial as the why, as this is a decisive motivating factor. It corresponds to a fundamental human need – our activities have to be meaningful we and we need to find confirmation in this. Therefore, meaning can also be described as a necessary pull factor for change projects.

Change process

Change means uncertainty. The home turf is abandoned while the new one is not yet "ready for occupancy". A well designed change process creates the necessary security at various levels.

From a purely operational point of view, it is important to flesh out and agree on the work packages and measures that are necessary to bridge the natural gap between the initial situation and the vision. In the case of the introduction of a contract management system, for example, various implementation packages were formulated, including the categorization of contracts, the development of a risk management logic, the development of a rights management, the creation of the necessary system and hardware environment, and finally the development of a training program for the operational users. To each of these work packages, a working group was assigned a task to develop their respective work package, taking into account the interfaces and interactions with the other work packages. These working groups were made up of mixed teams from the legal department and the operational units affected by the project. The procedure was chosen deliberately. The aim was to enable everyone to take ownership and thus increase acceptance of the system. The ultimate goal was to create a common understanding throughout the company of the importance of a contract management system for active risk management and their own contribution to it. The energy for change was relatively low at the beginning since the decision was predetermined and the software had already been chosen. In order to increase the commitment and the by-in in the goals of the project, it was therefore necessary to organize the most active participation possible and, above all, to encourage the operational managers to contribute to the success by taking on partial project responsibility.

As a general rule it can be said that the measures to be defined are to be customized for each project and, above all, they must be affordable in terms of time and money. In general, a high degree of involvement of those who are affected in other, mainly operational, units is helpful in change projects driven by legal departments; strong managers are very adept at effectively avoiding top-down approaches. They decide when they understand and are convinced – and they want to have a real decision respecting their self-image of their professional and managerial independence. Participation, however, always means extra work in addition to the day-to-day workload, from which there is de facto no release in such projects.

At the process architecture level, the organization, control, and mechanics of involvement and participation must also be defined for the project well in advance. This includes elements of classic project management, i.e., there is a project manager who coordinates the project including the sub-projects, checks the processing within the framework of time and budget, controls expenditure, reflects and determines the necessary steps with regard to the further procedure in terms of the objective, and ensures continuous communication. If there are sub-projects, they should be closely linked to the project management. Project management is a standard element in change processes. Its members must meet regularly.

The elements of involvement and participation must be tailored individually to the project, the legal department, and the company.

In legal departments, workshops are of particular importance, in which all those affected by the change are included. They have decisive advantages over the procedural model of classic management consultancies, the result of which is usually an externally formulated recommendation for action (although certainly tailored to the company being advised). Workshops, also tailored to large groups, on the other hand, are the most efficient way of working with precisely this resistance, using the energy to work out the best solution for the firm. Organizational conferences of this kind are much more than workshops, which are rather small settings and only allow a sequential approach. Large conferences drastically shorten the decision-making and information procedures through the simultaneity of information, processing, and decisions.[7] At the same time, the quality of the solutions is substantially increased.

Change projects in legal departments are often complex, as they have a cultural dimension as well as a strategic and structural one, especially when it comes to increasing the legal awareness of the top management team, their legal astuteness,[8] and making the rule of law the basic frame of all undertakings. Trivialization or quick solutions do not really help here either; rather, issues with conflicting interests require different perspectives, experiences, competencies, and ideas to achieve appropriate solutions.

As described in the case study, the process architecture for more extensive change projects provides for several large conferences, which are typically preceded by an evaluation (e.g., in the form of structured interviews) and an analysis. You can start, for example, with a "Future Conference" format, which is particularly suitable for designing the common future with a large group. These conferences create a sense of community, a spirit of optimism, and a high degree of motivation. The participants gain an understanding of their past, clearly recognize their present situation, and develop a common picture of the future. In the end, action plans for the unanimously chosen future are created. The action plans are then commonly deepened in smaller groups and brought back into the partnership in the form of soundings, where they are enriched (methodically, for example, in the form of a World Café or marketplaces) and worked out by smaller working groups until a decision is ready. Depending on the project, this may require several sequences in order to enable the partnership to become familiar with the change and actually adopt it.

Changes usually require different behavior from people than before. This does not happen automatically, but requires a longer period of time in which it is reflected again and again whether said change in behavior can be observed in the desired clarity. Some people will be able to implement this better than others and, if necessary, support them through individual promotion. The change process is only successful when the results of the implementation have solidified.

Leadership

Change projects place high demands on the leadership of the legal department. Leadership has the task of initiating change, defining the decision-making framework for the change project, winning powerful or dynamic stakeholders for the project, negotiating and enforcing budgets, organizing the process until it is commissioned, and dealing with resistance in the initial phase so that it does not nip the process in the bud.

The leadership in legal departments tends to be exercised not in a top down mode. This can have different reasons. One is certainly that leadership provided by legal professionals has a high degree of personal responsibility and at the same time a need for independence in their professional practice. The need for staff leadership is therefore often seen as lower than in other environments. Another reason is that leadership is rarely learned as a profession, with the theoretical background, methods, tools, and role clarity that comes with it. Thus, there is often a lack of understanding that to manage a legal department is a management task, and must also strive to strengthen legal in the company as a whole. Leadership here is provided laterally vis-à-vis the executive board and top management. If the general counsel has not been trained, it is advisable to support him specifically, e.g., through training, mentoring, or coaching, so that he becomes more capable of acting and is effectively available for any change project.

Conclusion

The in-house lawyers are only prepared to support changes if they have understood the necessity and the goal, i.e., the why and the what for, and have translated it into their own area of responsibility. In view of the cross-sectional function of the legal department, it is particularly important to include and involve the operational managers affected by the change project at an early stage. Legal departments are in general rather good at reacting quickly and flexibly to low-threshold adaptation and development requirements. If strategic undesirable developments in particular are systematically overlooked or the confrontation with early warning signs is avoided, it becomes increasingly difficult to change course. Patterns of conflict avoidance, consensus orientation, or the self-image of individual freedom of professionals are too deeply ingrained. At the beginning of the change process, the tendency to persist is particularly high in legal departments.

Change only has a chance of success if it is embedded in a binding process. It requires a kind of "initial spark" either from the legal management or from the board of directors. Top-down approaches or solution concepts developed from outside will otherwise have a hard time even getting into the implementation phase.

Involvement and participation formats such as large group settings are particularly effective methods that help to develop a common understanding of the initial situation and the vision and to operationalize the need for change. The phases of change processes can essentially be categorized as follows – the phase leading up to the commissioning of the change project, the development of answers and solutions to the challenges that need to be addressed and, last but not least, the implementation phase in which behavioral changes are practiced, consolidated, and secured. In each of these phases, the general counsel comes to lead the change project to success.

References

1 Based on Elfriede Jellinek in: Am Königsweg (textbook 2017).

2 Dannemiller, K. D., & Jacobs, R. W. (1992), Changing the way organizations change: A revolution of common sense. *The Journal of Applied Behavioral Science*, 28(4), 480–498): $C = D \times V \times F > R$ (C is change; D Dissatisfaction with how things are now; V Vision of what is possible; F First concrete steps that can be taken towards the vision. If the product of these three factors is greater than R Resistance then change is possible. Because D, V, and F are multiplied, if anyone is absent (zero) or low, then the product will be zero or low and therefore not capable of overcoming the resistance).

3 SWOT stands for Strengths, Weaknesses, Opportunities, Threats.

4 Specific, Measurable, Achievable, Reasonable, Time Bound.

5 Marvin Weisbord, *Future Search – An Action Guide to Finding Common Ground in Organizations and Communities*, 2010.

6 Visionsarbeit (Schulze, Henning: Visionsarbeit. In: Rohm, Armin [Hrsg.]: Change-Tools, 2020, S. 207ff).

7 S. Ruth Seliger, *Einführung in Großgruppen-Methoden*, 2015.

8 Constance E. Bagley, *Winning Legally: How To Use The Law To Create Value*, Marshal Resources, And Manage Risk, 2005.

About Globe Law and Business

Globe Law and Business was established in 2005. From the very beginning, we set out to create law books that are sufficiently high level to be of real use to the experienced professional, yet still accessible and easy to navigate. Most of our authors are drawn from Magic Circle and other top commercial firms, both in the United Kingdom and internationally.

Our titles are carefully produced, with the utmost attention paid to editorial, design and production processes. We hope this results in high-quality publications that are easy to read and a pleasure to own. Our titles are also available as ebooks, which are compatible with most desktop, laptop and tablet devices. In 2018 we expanded our portfolio to include journals and Special Reports, available both digitally and in hard copy format, and produced to the same high standards as our books.

In 2021, we were very pleased to announce the start of a new chapter for Globe Law and Business following the acquisition of law books under the imprint Ark Publishing. Our law firm management list is now significantly expanded with many well known and loved Ark Publishing titles.

We are also pleased to announce the launch of our online content platform, Globe Law Online. This allows for easy search and networked access across firms. Key collections include the Law Firm Management Collection, Private Client and Energy and the Energy Transition. Email me at sian@globelawandbusiness.com for further details or to arrange a free trial for you or your firm.

Sian O'Neill
Managing director
Globe Law and Business
www.globelawandbusiness.com

www.ingramcontent.com/pod-product-compliance
Ingram Content Group UK Ltd.
Pitfield, Milton Keynes, MK11 3LW, UK
UKHW021849150926
8657IPUK00005B/161

9 781787 428638